MW01136599

Kinderbeten

Kinderbeten

*The Origin, Unfolding, and Interpretations of the
Silesian Children's Prayer Revival*

Eric Jonas Swensson

WIPF & STOCK · Eugene, Oregon

KINDERBETEN
The Origin, Unfolding, and Interpretations of the Silesian Children's
Prayer Revival

Wipf & Stock
An Imprint of Wipf and Stock Publishers
199 W. 8th Ave., Suite 3
Eugene, OR 97401
www.wipfandstock.com

ISBN 13: 978-1-60608-864-7

Manufactured in the U.S.A.

To Joyce Y. Lewis Swensson, my precious pearl, without whose generosity and patience this work would not have been possible.

Wem ein tugendsam Weib bescheret ist, die ist viel edler denn die köstlichsten Perlen.
Proverbs 31:10

Contents

Abstract ix
Foreword xi
Introduction xiii

1   The Silesian People and Their Spirituality 1
2   The Kinderbeten 26
3   Pietist and Lutheran Orthodox 46
4   Conclusion 81

Bibliography 95

Abstract

THE ORIGIN of this revival came to be connected to the arrival of Swedish soldiers and their daily worship on the parade field, as both were seen providentially. Thus the prayer revival and the soldiers as an answer to prayers for liberation mutually informed one another in the minds of people in 1707–8. This was confused by the interpretation offered by Lutheran Orthodoxy that the revival had "mixed sources." Pietists, on the other hand, warmly embraced the movement and sought to place it within an apocalyptic interpretation of history, coming closer to the original conflation of the two events. However, both interpretations failed to give appropriate significance to reports that the revival had begun in the mountains before the Swedes' arrival.

It is suggested here that prayer is the key interpretive grid. Subsequent historians have missed this interpretation perhaps because of the presupposition against divine intervention. This is not to suggest that what follows is providential historiography; rather, it is necessary to acknowledge that people do act on the basis of their faith in order to see the whole picture of a religious movement. Evidence shows prayer meetings were common among Protestants in areas where religious freedom was repressed, a fact that has not been given enough weight by historians, perhaps by the easy solution offered by acceptance of the theory that the children imitated the Swedish soldiers. Importantly, all observers of the time failed to note the importance of the formative and activist nature of clandestine prayer meetings perhaps because of their predisposition toward providential historicism. That is, since Pietists assumed God was behind it other explanations were not sought, and detractors were most concerned that it could lead Enthusiasm, and neither would have looked for sociological factors as historians would today. Exercising their faith in prayer meetings was more than spiritual formation and a way for the *evangelische* Silesians to continue their Protestant beliefs. It was also a protest against oppression in their long yearning for a golden age. For their children, prayer meetings became an expression of grassroots social activism for religious freedom and peace.

Foreword

THE EXCITING events of the children's prayer meetings in
Silesia are well known in Germany as part of the early
history of Pietism, but they are much less well known in the
West than they should be, for they also form part of the early
history of that rather different thing, revivalism. For three different reasons I am happy to commend Mr. Swensson's account
of the movement. He has first managed to add a number of
points to earlier histories of the movement, which scholars in
the field should note. Second, churches are in various degrees
hierarchically organized and do not take kindly to nonhierar-
chical or antihierarchical movements like those here described.
The more recent confessions of Protestant church leaders that
in the late stages of the DDR they did not give enough attention
to the *Basisgruppen* come to mind. And third, there are important modern secular parallels to the story Mr. Swensson relates.
When the young people of Soweto concluded that no gains
were accruing to the compromising policies of their leaders,
rapid radicalisation followed. In short, Silesia in the late seventeenth and early eighteenth centuries offers food for thought to
everyone.

—W. R.Ward

Introduction

THE FIRST chapter of this book gives the general background on Silesia, its people, their religion, and the political-religious context before the Kinderbeten (praying children). The second is an examination of what was reported on the actual events based on the sources held at the Franckesche Stiftungen in Halle, Germany. This is followed by a close historical-theological reading of writings by three clergy who are representative of the different viewpoints involved: Pietist, Lutheran Orthodox, and radical Pietist. The last chapter is concerned with how the Kinderbeten reignited the controversy between Pietism and Orthodoxy and how this affected interpretations of the revival as well as how the two religious movements are understood up to today.

TALE OF HOPE AND PRAYER

Research into the roots of evangelicalism and revivalism uncovers its share of peculiarities, but nothing is more unusual than what follows. What is more, this is not an uncorroborated report about an isolated incident but a mass movement with a nation of eyewitnesses. Sometime in 1707 the children of Silesia began on their own to assemble in groups outdoors, two to three times a day to pray for freedom of religion and peace in their country. This began in the mountain villages of upper Silesia and spread down across the villages, towns, and cities of the entire nation. At morning, noon, and late afternoon the children of the community walked quietly two by two to a predetermined meeting place where they would sing a hymn, listen to a chapter of the Bible being read by one of their own, recite some psalms, and fall on their faces in prayer. Everything would come to a standstill as adults watched in wonder. This touched off a larger revival that endured for decades.[1] This was part of a process leading to the evangelization of neighboring states and the founding of the first Protestant denomination to have mission in the core of its identity, the Moravian church. Children's revivals erupted again and again in Protestant areas of the continent for decades,[2] including the Moravian Children's Revival in 1727, which is seen as one of their two main, formative events.[3] Soon enough the latter's members influenced the founders of new mission-minded movements, most famously John Wesley.

1. The terms "renewal" and "revival" are not used interchangeably here but follow W. Reginald Ward, *The Protestant Evangelical Awakening.* A. H. Francke's work is an example of renewal, and the Evangelical Silesian Praying Children's Awakening (*die evangelische schlesische Kinderbeten Erweckung*) would be an example of revival.

2. For example, compare this report from a remote mountain community in the parish of Bern to reports of the Silesian revival thirty years earlier: "Children there banded together to live a devout and loving life and seek Jesus. To this end they meet every morning and evening for prayer and singing. Some have an astonishing gift of prayer which cannot be observed without tears. They keep excellent order . . . the wildest children are becoming quiet refined lambs. No one has tried to persuade them into doing it, and they have such an impulse that they can scarcely wait for evening." *Sammlung auserlesener Materien zum Bau des Reiches Gottes,* 1044–5, as quoted in Ward, *Protestant Evangelical Awakening,* 182.

3. "Die Kindererweckung in Herrnhut im Jahre 1727 ist eines der Ereignisse in der Geschichte der Brüdergemeinde, das jedes Jahr mit einem eigenen Fest begangen wurde und wird: das Chorfest der Kinder, besonders der Mädchen am 17. August." Pia Schmid, "Die Kindererweckung in Herrnhut am 17. August 1727," in *Neue Aspekte der Zinzendorf-Forschung,* 115–33. Here and following, the German language sources are translated by myself and given in full in the footnote.

Why have we not heard of this before? As all but one of the reports of the period are in German, if not for the research of one historian, W. Reginald Ward, the Kinderbeten might still be unknown to the English-speaking world.[4] Second, it occurred in a country that was neither large nor powerful and no longer exists (the majority was annexed to Poland after World War II). Third, it happened among Lutherans, and revivalism is looked down on by the majority of Lutheran academics and clergy. Still, indulge your curiosity and read the remarkable story about the king of Sweden and the outbreak of the 1707–8 children's prayer revival in Silesia, a tale of hope and prayer.

A WORD ABOUT THE TERM "REVIVAL"

As in all Pietist circles, in the Silesian context an individual's conversion was called an "awakening" (*Erweckung*) and being awakened was understood as experiencing the regenerating work of the Holy Spirit and becoming a "new creation." In the following history let us be clear on what is *not* meant by revival when speaking of the events in Silesia. Marilyn J. Westerkamp, in *Triumph of the Laity*, defines "revivalism" as "rituals focused upon conversion and characterized by a highly charged emotional and physical, supposedly spontaneous, response to deliberate, organized efforts to stimulate that response."[5] We are not talking about that here; in fact, the lack of "deliberate, organized efforts" and the calm aspect (*stille*) of the children and their devotedness (*andächtig*) were highlighted by the adults who sought to understand it. The literature of the period discusses what kind of

---

4. These are but a few of the reasons the revival is unknown and may not even be the most important. Ward's 1992 work is the first to present these events in English since Increase Mather in 1709. Even in German, material on the revival since 1708–9 period is by the relatively few historians of *schlesische Kirchengeschichte*.

5. Westerkamp, *Triumph of the Laity*, 28.

movement (*Bewegung*) this was and no precedence is offered for this activity, with one exception.[6]

It was visited by throngs of adults who brought their own baggage as it unfolded. In one report passed on by a pastor of the Lutheran Orthodoxy, the people attending the children's prayer meetings were likened to "Quakers, Pietists, and Heathens," but it appears that they were painted by this broad brush principally because the meetings took place outdoors and without the benefit of being led by ordained clergy. (We will see there may be other reasons, political reasons, why outdoor meetings made the clergy nervous.) While the extremely organized Halle interests had a hand in the revival that was to follow, still one does not find organized activity aimed at mass conversions. What one finds is a total absence of organization in the children's revival, and in the concurrent and subsequent revival within Pietist congregations a simple methodology was followed of prayer and proclamation for the awakening of the parish one individual at a time and the inclusion of the awakened into the worship and discipleship life of the community.[7]

6. Johann Wilhelm Petersen mentions the Child Prophets of the Cevannes in *Die Macht der Kinder* as one of several movements which he mentions as proof that the last days were approaching.

7. To learn what revival looked like in Silesia in the decades that followed, see the description of the schedules of Pastor Schwedler in Nieder-Wiesa in *Quellenbuch zur Geschichte der evangelischen Kirche in Schlesien*, 177, and Pastor Sommer in Dirsdorf, Gerhard Meyer, *Gnadenfrei*, 37–8. For Schwedler's parish, prayer hours were held daily 5:00 a.m., noon, and 8:00 p.m. There were services and classes all day Sunday, and throughout the week a variety of classes were held in addition to prayer meetings and worship services. Sommer's schedule is perhaps the most revealing. When someone thought he or she had been "awakened," he or she came forward and pastoral care began. He or she could receive communion eight days later after special classes were taken. In addition to a full schedule of prayer meetings, Bible classes, etc., his wife led a meeting that taught the singing of hymns, and the pastors in the area met nightly in addition to their once a month conference. This

THE REPORTS FROM SILESIA

This work is based primarily on the published reports, letters, and judgments of evangelische Silesians and their neighbors in Germany. Eyewitness reports were circulated in letters and print by clergy and laymen who had created an informal, evangelical intelligence network between the continent, Great Britain, and its colonies. The reports began to circulate by means of an edition of *Europa Fama*,[8] an early newspaper of sorts, followed by *Gründliche Nachrichten,* a slender folio-sized book, which quoted the *Europa Fama* report and enlarged it with more eyewitness reports and judgments given by clergy and laity, even including what are said to be transcriptions of some of the children's prayers. Another source is *Acta Publica,* a large collection of various writings from 1707–8 concerning the Altranstädter Convention, and it includes a copy of *Gründlichen Nachrichten.* The main writings by clergy on the Kinderbeten are *Prüfung* by Johann Anastasius Freylinghausen and *Gutachten* by Caspar Neumann. *Die Macht der Kinder* by Johann Wilhelm Petersen contains references to the same.[9] *Gründliche Nachrichten* contains virtually all of the *Europa Fama* report, "Fernere Nachricht," *Gutachten*, a letter from Pastor Schindler signed by six other Silesian clergy, and two collections of prayers attributed to the children.[10] *Prüfung* is Freylinghausen's answer to Neumann's *Gutachten*. Silesian clergymen M. David Schindlers and M. Gottfried Balthasar

was in 1726. He was arrested in 1728 after being summoned to preach a sample sermon before the Consistory.

8. *Euröpäischeshen FAMA*, indem 74, 114–34.

9. Two others not commented on due to space limitations are "Die Andacht Betender Kinder in Schlesien" by M. Gottfried Balthasar Scharffen and "Zuschrifft An die benachbarte Priesterschafft Um Einhaltung Des Zulauffs derer Kinder zum ausserordentlichen Gebet" by M. David Schindlers.

10. The title page of *Gründliche Nachrichten* could lead you to believe it was written by Neumann but means a copy of *Gutachten* is included.

Scharffen also wrote judgments, but they did not receive the same attention at the time and are less interesting than the above. Furthermore, word of the revival disseminated into the English-speaking world through "Praise out of the Mouths of Babes,"[11] which was also based on *Europa Fama* combined with additional material. These reports from Silesia are discussed in the second chapter of this work, and the writings by the clergy representing the three schools of thought are in the third.

REPRESENTATIONS (DARSTELLUNG)

Pictures are worth thousands of words. As representations of ideas, they usher the viewer into a particular world. The engravings found on the title pages of two histories offered at the spring Frankfurt book fair of 1708 convey the viewer into two separate but linked dramatic events. The first is a negotiation between two monarchs instigated by a political-military gamble, one of which resulted in a degree of religious freedom in a time of persecution (see fig. 1). The second is an account of the Silesian Children's Prayer Revival (fig. 2 is the cover of *Gründliche Nachrichten*). The two are similar in appearance and could almost be by the same illustrator, though the second artist could well be imitating the first. That would be fitting because all reports of the time pass along the theory that the children were copying the Swedish soldiers' way of having morning and evening prayer. It is proposed here that the two events were most definitely related, but until the connection is made between the hope that springs from answered prayer (what fig. 1 represents) and the additional prayer

11. *Praise out of the Mouth of Babes: or a Particular Account of Some Extraordinary Pious Motions and Devout Exercises, Observed of Late in Many Children in Silesia*. Three versions are available on microfilm: the 1708 by Downing, one published by Increase Mather in Boston in 1709, and another edition printed in Boston in 1741.

that hope generates (fig. 2), a possible origin of the Kinderbeten revival has been overlooked.

Both engravings are rich in symbolic meanings as well as including the actual people and events. Both feature two oval-shaped portraits, with Emperor Joseph I on the left and Karl XII, the young and ambitious soldier-king of Sweden, on the right. Figure 1 has the portraits suspended in the sky over a stormy sea. Figure 2 has them imposed on a landscape with mountains in the background and a scene of village life in the foreground. Top center in both is that strange image found on the back of the U. S. dollar bill, an eye within a pyramid, which represents the Trinity and symbolizes how God had been listening to the prayers of the Silesian faithful and watching as events had unfolded and had at last chosen to answer them and intervene on their behalf.

Figure 1 conveys little information concerning Karl XII's surprise appearance with forty thousand soldiers near the border with Austria; rather, it is a commemoration of what led to and came out of the negotiation at the Altranstädter Convention where on September 6, 1707, Joseph I chose to return 120 of the 1,200 evangelische churches confiscated in the Counter-Reformation and allowed for some additional free exercise of religion. Below the two large oval portraits of the royal adversaries, Catholic on the left and Evangelical Lutheran on the right, we find the insertion of two round depictions. Around the one on the left is written *suum cuique*, "To each their own," referring to the policy of *Cuius regio, eius religio*, the all-important guiding principle in the struggle of the Germanic princes, and as we shall see, one of the key factors in not only the continual negotiations between Catholic, Lutheran, and Reformed but also a convenient tool to marginalize any other expressions of Christianity. Around the second depiction are the words *benedictus dominus*, "Blessed be the Lord," an acknowledgment that God was to be praised for what had happened. These small insertions serve to illustrate the relation of hope to prayer.

The picture on the left shows six hands raised up through the clouds and one hand reaching down as if to clasp them. This represents the rising up of intercessory prayer. The picture on the right shows the children of Israel carrying the ark of the covenant toward Jerusalem, except this Zion is Breslau, the capital of Silesia. This represents answered prayer. Between that scene and the portrait of Karl is written, "The joy of the Evangelische Silesians over obtaining religious freedom."[12] In between the two circles is the focus of the all-seeing eye, a little boat on a stormy sea. The boat is reminiscent of a scene found on church stained-glass windows, the story of the disciples who became terrified of a storm while crossing the Sea of Galilee. Boats have long been symbolic of the Church. The words above this boat read, "Fear not . . ." and underneath, "The Lord helps . . ."[13] Two verses of poetry show how the monarchs' roles were understood by the evangelische. From the verse under the portrait of Joseph I:

> Oh, Israel storms heaven with praying, until GOD and
> the emperor tread on the enemies.[14]

Under the portrait of Karl XII:

> Receive, O Lord, your people by such strong power,
> courage, good, and prosperity, can truly offer.[15]

12. This artwork is used opposite the title page in Norbert Conrads, *Die Durchführung der Altranstädter Konvention in Schlesien.* "Der Evangelischen Schlesier Freude uber erhaltene Religions Freyheit" (fig. 1).

13. The quote reads, "Fürchet Euch . . . Herr hilff uns wir verderben." Ibid.

14. "Wer ist gnädiger nach Seiner Aart zu preisen, Als GOTT im Himmel ist, und Joseph auf der Welt
Wo diese Aüg und Hand dem Unterthanen weisen, Da ist so Kirch und Hauß in allem wohl bestellt.
Ach Israel stürme den Himmel mit bethen, Bis GOTT und der Kaiser die Feinde zutreten." Ibid.

15. "Erhalt, o Herr, dein Volck bey solche starcke Kräffte, Daß es Muth, Güt und Blüt getreulich opffern kan. So wird man eine Schrifft an

Figure 2 is laid out like the first. Whereas figure 1 was purely commemorative, figure 2 includes actual events under symbolic images. Rays stream out of the all-seeing eye as in figure 1, but in figure 2 it is a beam focused straight downward on a mountain. This is significant and an important piece of information about the origin of the revival, that is, "everyone knew that the prayer revival began in the *Gebirge*," the mountainous region of Upper Silesia.[16] At bottom center is another boat on stormy sea with the words, "Fear not." Where there were round pictures below the oval portraits in the first, there are two circles made up of kneeling figures with a leader in the center of each. Scattered groups of adults look on with some gesturing toward the children, and others appear to be talking.

Figure 1 illustrates how the evangelische Silesians understood the first event, that God had answered their prayers. For over fifty years they had been under harsh oppression from the Hapsburgs who used Jesuits in an aggressive campaign of re-Catholization. Some of the evangelische clergy did not obey the expulsion at the time of confiscation and instead hid in the mountains and became clandestine preachers (*Buschprediger*). They urged their flocks to read their Bibles, sing their hymns, and pray to God for strength to endure until their prayers were answered.

Help did arrive in the late summer of 1707 in the form of Karl XII and his soldiers. Everyone, Silesians, Swedes, allies, and opponents, understood that the king of Sweden had assumed the role of Gustavus Adolphus, protector of the evangelische faith, a right stipulated in the Treaty of Westphalia. When word circulated that Karl XII's emissaries had successfully negotiated the

---

Sales sfoste hefften. Der Wunderbare GOtt hat Wunder hier gethan.

So wird man bey Kirche und Schulen, sich freüen, Daß GOtt und Kayser und Freyheit verleihe." Ibid.

16. Gerhard Eberlein, "Die schlesischen Betekinder vom Jahre 1707/8." In: *Evangelisches Kirchenblatt für Schlesien. Zweiter Jahrgang*," 74–6, here 52.

return of their churches, Silesians were exceedingly overjoyed. They wrote poetry and songs and struck commemorative medals, comparing Karl XII not only to Gustavus Adolphus but also to other soldier kings such as Alexander the Great and King David.[17] It is clear from the two figures as well as from all the reports that God was understood to be the source of that help. (Presumably the Roman Catholics would disagree!)

It is also clear that lay people and historians alike living before the Enlightenment had a providential understanding of history and some historians continued this view into the nineteenth century, but clearly historians since then do not. One must take great care in analyzing the reports. It has already been noted that the evangelische reported that God sent the Swedish army to Silesia. What do we do with the other providentialist reports? It was said that the prayer revival began in the *Gebirge,* that it moved down and spread to five principalities within five days, and that this rapid dispersion began on December 28, Holy Innocents Day. This is an example of the providential view of history that pervades the accounts. Obviously everything has to be treated objectively. We will endeavor to do so but to not belabor every point.

It was commonly reported that the children were copying the Swedish soldiers who formed circles by regiment for morning and evening prayer. However, it was also communicated without comment how the prayer movement began among the children of the *Gebirge.* Of all the reports concerning the nature and origin of the revival, these are the two events that will serve as the main historiographical markers. Why is this question of origin an interesting question? Not only was the *Gebirge* an area where the children did not have the opportunity to see the Swedes, as it was not on the route of the soldiers' march, but it was also the area that had the most severe oppressions. Most historians of

17. See Dietrich Meyer, "Die Auswirkungen der Altranstädter Konvention auf die evangelische Kirche Schlesiens und die Bewegung der betenden Kinder," a chapter in an upcoming book commemorating the treaty, received from the author electronically, 09/15/2008.

the last century who have written about the Kinderbeten do not give enough weight to the fact that evangelische worship would necessarily be clandestine in an area where it is proscribed. Furthermore, would clandestine meetings not consist of Bible reading, proclamation, hymn singing, and prayer? Would this not be an alternative pattern for the children's devotion? And is not an earnest prayer meeting focused on liberation from oppression essentially activist-oriented? Considering that the children had probably imbibed their parents' prayers for peace and freedom in this manner, is this not a more likely pattern? When the children took their prayer meetings to the streets was it not in fact a form of protest against the powers that be?

Except for Dietrich Meyer's article in 2008, historical accounts since Gerhard Eberlein's from 1899 usually only refer to the *Gutachten* of Caspar Neumann, someone who writes from the perspective of Lutheran Orthodoxy, and do not give any evidence of an investigation of the Pietists' writings of the period, such as *Prüfung* or *Die Macht der Kinder*.[18] Historians pass on the story of the children copying the Swedish soldiers unchallenged. G. Eberlein reports the children in the *Gebirge* did not see the Swedes and began their prayer meetings at the beginning of the summer of 1707 before the Swedes made their surprise march. Why did this cease to be of interest? Was it that an explanation for the Kinderbeten was needed that was suitable to such a peculiar event, something dramatic yet reasonable? Thus it made sense to say that the children's public prayer meetings were simply impressionable children copying the dashing soldiers. However, we cannot use Eberlein's report of 1899 uncritically. Eberlein based this at least partially on C. A. Schmmelpfennig's 1868 Silesian church history work, where surprisingly the quote came from Caspar Neumann himself, someone who gave a mixed review of the revival and did not seem to give much importance to anything to do with the origination of the revival.[19]

18. See note 2, chapter 2.

19. "Ueber Ort und Tag seiner Entstehung fehlen alle zuverlässigen

To conclude the introduction, the Silesian Kinderbeten Revival came to be connected to the presence of Karl XII's Swedish soldiers because their arrival was also seen as a providential event. Thus the prayer revival and the presence of the Swedish army as an answer to prayers for liberation mutually informed one another in the minds of contemporaries. Still, this connection was confused by the interpretations of Lutheran Orthodoxy, which said that because of the presence of certain practices the devil and human artifice were also involved. Pietists, on the other hand, warmly embraced the movement and sought to place it within an apocalyptic interpretation of history. Thus the Pietist view seems to be closer to the original conflation of the two events (revival and Swedes) because these two events were read in light of an apocalypticism that had a strong view of the intervention of divine providence. Nevertheless, both groups failed to give appropriate significance to reports that the revival had begun in the mountains before the Swedes' arrival.

It is suggested here that established practices of prayer is the key interpretive grid, not providential history or merely children imitating soldiers. Subsequent historians missed the interpretation possibly because of presuppositions against divine intervention, but another reason for the transmission of the theory that the children copied the soldiers is that it is an easy solution to what would appear to be a conundrum for historians who need evidence and empirically based arguments. However, one does not need to engage in providential historiography to explain the origin of the revival. A more plausible

---

Nachrichten. Nach Walch (Rel.-Str. der ev. luth. K. I. S. 853) datirt es aus dem October 1707 und Anders (Hist. Statistik S. 36) nennt Sprottau als den Ort, wo es seinen Anfang genommen haben soll. Nach Caspar Neumann hingegen ‚ist fast den ganzen Sommer 1707 durch die Kinder im Gebirge, auch an etlichen Orten im Glogauschen Fürsten thum schon gebetet worden.' Diese unbestimmten Nachrichten beweisen hinlänglich, daß man anfangs „aus diesem Beten nicht gar viel gemachet," sondern es mehr als Spielwerk betrachtet hat. Erst als es sich weiter ausbreitete und Aufsehen erregte, wurde es mit dem Nimbus einer göttlichen Erweckung umkleidet."

argument than mere imitation of the Swedish soldiers is being offered here. What has been overlooked is the evidence that shows that prayer meetings were common among the evangelische in Hapsburg-occupied Silesia.[20] The children's prayer meetings were not an entirely new phenomenon but an adaptation. We can surmise that the children who began the prayer meetings had learned to pray this way by imitating their parents, not the Swedish soldiers, as the latter has not arrived yet. Only after the soldiers' arrival could the children have been influenced by the soldiers, at which time they were probably influenced by both. There were two features of the children's prayer revival that were new: the size of the meetings and that the children were meeting without any adult leadership.

However, everything was clouded by the interpretation offered by Caspar Neumann. As the head clergyman of the evangelische in the capital city of Silesia and recognized as the leader throughout the country, he was, after all, responsible for their general well-being as well as having to answer to the authorities. He had good reason to downplay the revival because of the danger of repercussions from the Hapsburg Empire. Beginning sixty years earlier, the Hapsburgs had closed over twelve hundred evangelische churches and exiled the pastors and their families. Memories of the horrible war still lingered. Neumann therefore would not have been the person to direct a searchlight into areas of the country where the practice of the evangelische faith was in fact illegal. He mentioned the origin once. Neumann, the person everyone would have looked to for a judgment on the revival was a clergyman who, for his whole career, had to work under Catholic authorities who had the power to turn his homeland into another Bohemia and Moravia. Therefore the Orthodox reaction to the revival is never as black and white as it might seem, and this needs to be kept in mind while probing what has been said on the origin of the revival and the role the Kinderbeten played in creating controversy between Lutheran Orthodoxy and the Pietist clergy. While reaction of the

20. Herbert Patzelt's work, for example. See chapter 1, note 42.

orthodox clergy gives us an interesting entrance into theological controversies still with us today, nothing is as simple as it seems.

Ironically, providentialist history and contemporary historians both point to the arrival of the Swedish soldiers for instigating the Kinderbeten, and both fail to recognize the importance of the ongoing clandestine prayer meetings by the oppressed evangelische. The alternative view provided by this thesis is that the key is what came before; the children would have attended prayer meetings, as it were, on their parents' knees.

This tale of hope and prayer begins with an effort to obtain a clearer picture of the faith of the people at that time in history in that part of the world. These were a people who had long desired and acted for reform of church and society. In their own way, Silesians prefigured the Reformation and the Pietist movement (though there were clear differences between the Hussites and the Lutherans). It is impossible to reach any definite conclusions about the illegal Protestant cell churches without locating the primary sources concerning them, but what we do know is very interesting. We look at those sources now.

1

The Silesian People and Their Spirituality

HISTORICAL BACKGROUND

NO LONGER on the map, a casualty of war, Silesia was from ancient times a nation located south of Saxony and Prussia, southwest of Poland, east of Bohemia and Moravia, and north of Austria and Hungary. That and what follows is an effort to simplify a complicated map of a time, place, the faith of its people and their political and religious institutions, and how a pietistic prayer revival was birthed and spread abroad. One could have guessed the country's fate was to be traded one too many times because, "Silesia always had an overlord."[1]

Two things need to be mentioned about beliefs and spirituality in the general historical background of the Kinderbeten: nothing definite can be said about spiritual movements before the Reformation due to the paucity of historical evidence, and while we know the Hussite movement spread into Silesia and continued to exert influence, it was an undercurrent, a clandestine influence, because of the fear of reprisal.[2] However, "In each spiritual movement that went through the German Church, Silesia had its share."[3] Most of these movements ran into opposi-

1. "Schlesien hat immer Oberhaubt," Eberlein, *Schlesische Kirchengeschichte*, 15.

2. Interview with Dietrich Meyer, September 15, 2008.

3. "An allen geistlichen Bewegungen, die durch die deutschen

1

tion and in some cases the harshest persecution, which did
not eradicate any of them and at times may have led to their
growth. The rise of a vision for reform in the Church, opposi-
tion, and further work for reform became the pattern for Silesia:
Waldensian, Hussite, *Unitas Fratrum*, Anabaptist, evangelische
Lutheran, Schwenkfelder, Reformed, Pietist, Moravian, etc.
Being oppositional, always in tension with the establishment, is
one of the characteristics of lay spiritual movements such as the
one in Silesia at the time of the outbreak of the Kinderbeten.[4] The
Waldensians' growth in the first half of the fourteenth century
was seen in its persecution: no less than fifty men, along with
their wives and children, were burned at the stake.[5] Attempts by
the Inquisition to weed out the Waldensians in the fourteenth
and fifteenth centuries failed, and there was a report of a large
Waldensian "migration" through Silesia in 1480.[6]

Kirchen gingen, hatte Schlesien seinen Anteil." Eberlein, *Schlesische
Kirchengeschichte*, 90. Eberlein includes the *Geißelbrüder* in 1261 and
1349, 33.

4. Lay Pietism (*Laienpietismus*) is based on simple trust in the Bible
as the ground of belief, centers on the need for rebirth, and is biblicist,
idealist, experiential, and oppositional. See *Charismatic Christianity as
a Global Culture*, xii. I would add that it has an emphasis on prayer, and
all five characteristics come from a plain reading of the Bible.

5. For one school of thought on dissenting groups such as
Waldensians, see Knox, *Enthusiasm*, a well-researched book with
a wealth of information. The only thing one can be certain of is that
anything that is not Roman Catholic is heretic to Monsignor Knox,
who went so far as to suggest (this I say partially tongue-in-cheek) that
certain regions of the world were heretic. It is to say that a historian
cannot accept a label being applied to a group without a credible
primary source at hand; all one may be certain of when reading about a
marginal group is that they were marginalized.

6. "In Fulneck im Kuhländchen wurden sie 1480 durch die
Zuwanderung von Waldesern aus Neumark verstark." Patzelt, *Pietismus
im Teschener* 19.

There was an apocalyptic impulse running through these movements, but it was not about standing in a field while waiting for the New Jerusalem to come down from the sky. Rather these were biblically informed, action-oriented movements aimed at reforming the Church and society. The Hussite cause began as a reformation of the Church, but in hindsight it became a societal revolution leading to protracted war with the Empire from 1419 to 1436.[7] Through the centuries, dissenters would point to the Bible as the proof of their truth, which is another key to lay spiritual movements. One motto of the Hussittes was, "Truth wins." Another found on their shields and banners was "the golden dream" (i.e., the thousand-year eschatological kingdom).[8] Their desire for reform had a biblical-apocalyptic edge to it.

The Hussites originated in Bohemia, and their influence spread to the other regions of the Bohemian crown, Moravia, and Silesia. They were a movement sparked by the transmission of the writings of the English reformer John Wycliffe (1320–84). One follower, Wiklift Stephan, was burned at the stake in Breslau, the capital of Silesia, 1398, seventeen years before Jan Hus (1372–1415) met the same end at Constance. Hus was a leader of a broad church reform movement within the ranks of nobles, clergy, students, merchants, artisans, and farmers that was already concerned with reform of the Church before they

7. Patzelt, *Geschichte der Evangelischen Kirche in Österreichisch-Schlesien*, 13.

8. "Veritas Vincit, so stand es im Wappen der ersten Tschechoslowakischen Republik. Es ist der Wahlspruch der hussitischen Revolution des. Jahrhunderts, die sich gegen den Zerfall der Sitten in hoher und niedriger Geistlicher wandte, sich in Haß gegen Herrschende und Besitzende steigerte, soziale Ungerechtigkeit bekämpfte und entäuscht war über den Mangel an Unterstützung durch den Kaiser. In Bühmen blühte zu dieser Zeit eine apokalytische Erwartung, das Tausendjährige Reich war ein goldener Traum." Herbert Patzelt, "Die böhmischen Brüder und ihre Beziehungen zu Deutschland." In: *Kirchen und Bekenntnisgruppen im Osten des Deutschen Reiches*, 47.

read Wycliffe. Whereas Luther's writings were primarily theological (though used by others for political ends), the primary interest of Hus was the need to reform church practices. This yearning for reform continued to exist throughout the different time periods of the historical background of the Kinderbeten. For example, the *Unitas Fratrum,* of which Comenius was the last bishop, made its imprint on spiritual life in Silesia from 1457 through the seventeenth century. There was a similarity between the piety of the *Unitas Fratrum* and the Pietists who came later.[9] What was left of it to be "renewed" by Zinzendorf and how much at Berthelsdorf was a new creation is an interesting question for further research.[10]

The negative effects of the war only exacerbated the fact that Silesians were affected by the same reform currents swirling through Europe, seen in a rise in repentance preaching, clergy reform, and the intellectual reform movement called Humanism. In 1467 a papal legate came from Germany to bring more order to a church whose people had experienced seventeen years of

9. "Trotz manch Änlichkeit und Praxis der alten Brüderunität sahen sie bei den Pietisten einen grundverschiendenen Unterschied. Die Frömmigkeit der Brüderunität kannte nicht dieses In-sich-selbst-vertieft-Sein; sie beschäftigen sich nicht so mit ihrer eigenen Person. Nicht einmal Comenius, obwohl er in dieser werden . . . Dafür fand die neue pietistiche Frömmigkeit immer neue tapfere Männer, die ihr Leben wagten, um den Gläubigen durch ihre Predigt zu helfen und sie im Glauben zu stärken." Patzelt, "Die böhmischen Brüder," 61.

10. Even a cursory comparison of the interview with Christian David and other founders of Herrnhut by John Wesley in his journal and the history Zinzendorf gave on his passing in 1751 (found in *Christian David, Servant of the Lord*) shows that Zinzendorf saw things one way and David another. Since Zinzendorf "had his fingers in everything," it is reasonable to assume that shaping the faith, its propaganda, and its history is included in that. One wonders if the faith of many of the people in what was essentially a lay movement was not much more a Jesus-based generic Protestantism rather than a denomination always following the idiosyncratic lead of Zinzendorf. Wesley surely would have used it after his later problems with Moravians in England.

brutal war. Living through confessional intolerance led to a new spirit in the people toward openness.[11] There was a general outcry against the "offensive life" of clergy as seen in the 1524 public denunciation of "*das Trio*": gambling, drinking, and concubines.[12] Repentance preachers like John of Capistrano (d. 1456) were also in the foreground of the pre-Reformation picture. Humanism was more than an infatuation with language; Erasmus and others were calling for Church reform. The younger generation of Silesian clergy joined the Humanist movement en masse. The greater emphasis on learning Greek and Hebrew prepared the intellectual ground for the Reformation. Schwenkfeld and Crautwald, who were to lead the Schwenkfelder movement originating in Silesia, were part of a Humanist circle whose intellectual exploration led to a new teaching on Christology, the sacraments, ecclesiology, and a journey back into mystical spirituality.

THE REFORMATION

As Helmut Eberlein said, "The time of John the Baptist has passed, the time of the Gospel approaches."[13] The ground in Silesia was warm and fertile for receiving the seed of Luther's teachings on faith.[14] Concerning the arrival of the Reformation, one Silesian historian wrote, "That indulgence preacher Tetzel was not unknown in Silesia and so the herald's call from Wittenberg found

11. Patzelt, *Evangelischen Kirche in Österreichisch-Schlesien*, 14.

12. "Die kirchlichen Synodalakten bestätigen das traurige Bild. Denn „Spieler, Trinker und Konkubinarier bilden das Trio, gegen das Synode um Synode ankämpft" und die Breslauer Gesandten hatten schon ihre Gründ, auf dem Grottkraür Fürstentage von 1524 öffentliche Klage zu erheben: „Etliche Praelaten haetten zwar kein ehelichen Weiber, verführten aber Bürgern ihre Ehofraün und brächten ihre Toechter zu Schaden . . ." Eberlein, *Schlesische Kirchengeschichte*, 36.

13. "Die Zeit Johannes des Täufers, die Zeit des Evangeliums brach an," 39.

14. Ibid.

open ears and hearts in our homeland."[15] Another historian echoed this, stating, "The Reformation had found in Silesia open doors and hearts, so that the whole country including Upper Silesia for the predominant part was attached to the new teaching."[16] The Wittenberg Reformation was a kindred movement to what was already taking place in Silesia (as we shall soon see, Halle Pietism was "a kindred spirit" to the spirituality in Silesia at the time of Children's Awakening in 1707).[17] In 1521, within a half year of the formation of an evangelische party in the Breslau Cathedral, a Canon there described the Silesian situation to Rome:

> The number of confessions decreases, there's no more care for religion, no reverence for the priesthood, no fear of a penalty from the Church! The authority of the clerics is low, barely there, especially for the Roman See. And where does all of this come from? There: Luther's books are read without punishment, endlessly printed and translated in each language! With approval, yes, all the people take with joy that which comes from Luther. All give themselves out as Lutherans; truly the name Christian is obsolete. Luther is on each tongue, that is certain.[18]

15. "Die Heroldsrufe von Wittenberg in unserer Heimat offene Ohren und Herzen fanden, zumal ja der Ablaßprediger Tetzel den Schlesiern kein Unbekannter war." Ibid., 41.

16. "Die Reformation hatte in Schlesien offene Türen und Herzen gefunden, so daß das ganze Land einschließlich Oberschlesiens zum überwiegenden Teil der neuen Lehre anhing." Meyer, *Gnadenfrei*, 9.

17. "Wir dürfen die Bewegungen der betenden Kinder als eine Massenbewegung ansehen, die dem Pietismus verwandt ist und besonders das einfache Volk ihm erschliesst." Ibid., 17.

18. "Die Zahl der Beichtenden nimmt ab, keine Pflege der Religion mehr, keine Ehrfurcht von dem Priesterstande, keine Furcht vor Kirchenstrafe! Die Autorität des Klerus ist dahin, nicht bloß die des niederen, sondern sogar die des Römischen Stuhles. Und woher alles? Daher: Luthers Bücher würden straflos gelesen, endlos gedruckt und in

They did embrace the teachings of Luther; nonetheless, there was some independence from the person of Luther. The Silesians had watched the persecution of Hussites and learned the hard way to be wary of identification with controversial figures, perhaps to nuance things. However, their historians report that their spirituality was more in tune with Melanchthon. Or perhaps there was another reason for maintaining some distance. In 1523 Friedrich II, the count of Liegnitz, the most important of Silesian principalities at the time, wrote a "letter of warning" to the Polish King Sigismund, explaining the changes taking place in the land under his rule, that "nothing but the Holy Gospel is preached, and nothing but the Word of God, without Luther or the addition of any human words."[19] It was declared in Breslau in 1524 that "where Luther and his books are mentioned, it should be seen that one has accepted the Word of God, not the person [of Luther]."[20] Humanist Lorenz Corvin, one of the Silesians responsible for the introduction of the evangelische faith, wrote in a letter in 1525 that one should see to it that one teaches Christ's teachings and not Luther's or Zwingli's.[21]

Before the 1580 "Visitation of Breslau Bistums" and the beginning of the return of some of the nobility to Roman

---

jede Sprache übersetzt! Mit Beifall, ja, mit Frohlocken nehme das Volk alles auf, was von Luther kommt. Alle geben sich für Lutheraner aus, während der Christenname veralte. Luther sei in all Munde, das stehe fest." Eberlein, *Schlesische Kirchengeschichte*, 42.

19. "Friedrich II. versicherte Ende 1523 dem polnischen Koenig Sigismund auf dessen Warnungschreiben, daß in seiner Landeshauptmannschaft nichts anderes als das heilige Evangelium und lautere Gotteswort ohne Luthers und sonst menschlichen Zusatz." Ibid., 43.

20. "Würde Luthers und seiner Bücher gedacht, so sei zu antworten, man habe nichts damit zu schaffen; schreibe aber Luther dem Worte Gottes gemaeß, so habe man das Wort Gottes angenommen, nicht die Person." Ibid.

21. Ibid., 44.

Catholicism,[22] the two Confessions, Catholic and evangelische, had peaceful relations.[23] Perhaps that was because it was such a sudden and lopsided conversion as 90 percent of Silesia became evangelische. The starting date for the official beginning of the evangelische church in Breslau is 1525, and it happened without any large tumult. It was established in Teschen in 1528 where by 1536 the Franciscans left of their own free will, followed by the Dominicans in 1545.

According to Eberlein, it was a conservative Reformation as far as retaining outward ceremonial practices; until the end of the eighteenth century exorcism and immersion of infants in baptism was kept, as well as the elevation of bread and wine, private confession, the priests' vestments, genuflection, etc. In principalities like Teschen the counts issued church decrees that introduced the reforms suggested by Philipp Melanchthon's 1528, "Der Unterricht der Visitation." The early institution of Sunday catechetical sermons and regular weekly sermons on Wednesdays and Fridays, and children's education in evangelische teachings, shows the Reformation was introduced by systematic teaching of adults and children. The *Landeskirche* can also be seen as theologically conservative in that while they embraced reform they did not move toward antinomianism or a predominately intellectual understanding. According to Christian-Erdmann Schott, Silesia had from early times influential evangelische preachers like Abraham Buchholzer (1529–84),

22. Helmut Eberlein gives the impression of an earlier commencement to the Counter-Reformation than Herbert Patzelt. One of the first things one notices in Eberlein's timeline for the Reformation is the early end date (1580) because of the re-Catholization instigated by the bishop of Breslau. Patzelt, whose focus is Teschen, quotes the 1610 report of George Fabricius that there was "full harmony between the two Confessions" (*daß zwischen beiden Gemeinden volle Harmonie herrsche*).

23. See Meyer, "Pietismus im Schelsien," 20. Also, "Das Verhältniss der beiden Konfessionen zu einander war harmonisch und friedlich." Meyer, *Gnadenfrei*, 9.

a student of Melanchthon who emphasized the application of biblical texts to daily life, and he was the father of a movement marked by a "Silesian sensitivity," different from Schwenkfelder and radicals in their orientation to a consciousness of the application of the message on the members of a church.[24] These early influential preachers had a close connection to Humanism and thought of themselves as teachers. They were "Melanchthonirenic." Therefore, the Silesian church was a Melanchthon variety of Lutheranism,[25] which meant, among other things, that they did not go in for dogmatic denunciations of the Reformed and Papists. In these two areas they prefigured Spener's reform principles in Germany. As a whole, the *Landeskirche* had a predisposition to a moderate churchly pietism.

SCHWENKFELD, CRAUTWALD, AND THE SCHWENKFELDER MOVEMENT

Kaspar von Schwenkfeld (1489–1561) served in the court of Count Friedrich II, the principality of Liegnitz, from 1518 to 1523

24. "Buchholzer hatte nämlich erkannt, dass man die Bibel nicht nur korrekt auslegen, sondern die Auslegung auch so applizieren muss, dass die Leute sich dem Aufruf zum Tun des Gehörten nicht entziehen können. Darum hat er seine Predigten regelmäßig in Gebete ausklingen lassen, in denen die Gemeinde darum bittet das Gehörte nun auch mit Gottes Hilfe im Alltag umzusetzen." Schott, "Der Pietismus in Schlesien.," Meyer, Schott, and Schwarz, *Über Schlesien Hinaus: Zur Kirchengeschichte in Metteleuropa, Festgabe für Herbert Patzelt zum 80. Geburstag*, 129.

25. "Damit ist Buchholzer der Vater einer Bewegung, die ich als die schlesische Innerlichkeit bezeichne. Im Unterschied zu den Schwenkfeld und zur radikalen Mystik ist die schlesische Innerlichkeit auf die Landeskirche orientiert und bewusst auf die Kirchenmitglieder bezogen. Sie ist gelehrt, gebildet und legt Wert auf ihre enge Bindung an den Humanismus. Das heißt: Sie ist humanistisch. Und sie ist Melanchthonisch-irenisch. Man hielt sie für lutherisch, tatsächlich war sie eine Melanchthonische Variante des Luthertums." Ibid.

and played a role in the introduction of the Reformation there. He had embraced the teachings of Luther but soon developed his own understanding. His innovations led to his voluntary exile in 1529. He had a long career, journeying from controversial character to persecuted radical. Having found a friendly home in Augsburg, he soon enough had to leave. Schwenkfeld spent years traveling through southern Germany, visiting cell groups he had helped found, but his last years were as a fugitive.

Since Schwenkfeld came to believe that one could not rely on proclamation of the word to effect justification, or Luther's teaching on the real presence of Christ in the Lord's Supper, Lutheran word and sacrament ministry was to him essentially inconceivable. He looked for the fruit of reform in the life of Lutherans, did not see it, and decided that Luther did not go far enough. He did not return to Silesia. Nevertheless, a movement was shaped by his writings that existed in Silesia until the 1830s (the group that immigrated to Pennsylvania in 1740 still exists).

Valentin Crautwald (1465–1545), a colleague of Schwenkfeld, began as a canon theologian, became a major Spiritualist figure, and is just as important to the development of the movement's theology as the man for whom it is named.[26] As he was not exiled he was able to remain and influence the movement. Crautwald began as a cautious reformer, influenced by Erasmus, Zwingli, and Melanchthon. His ideas continued in the Humanist vein even as he became thoroughly Spiritualist. It was not until September 1525 that Crautwald came to these ideas through a "conversion." This was a short time after Schwenkfeld brought him the *Duodecium Questiones* (*Twelve Questions*), a foundational document for the Schwenkfelder movement, where one sees Zwinglian emphases—the need to guard the honor of Christ as the only source of salvation and faith as the only means—but it goes further in stating the need to identify the ground for holding to the importance of the glorified body

26. Shantz, *Crautwald and Erasmus*.

of Christ.[27] By placing importance on the partaking of the glorified body and stressing the necessity of faith, such great influence was placed on the hidden and internal and disregard shown to the external that the direction was already set for the *Stillestand*, the Schwenkfelder exception to the Lord's Supper. Crautwald had been appointed Lector, first at the cathedral and then the University of Liegnitz, and when Schwenkfeld went into exile, the more reserved Crautwald was able to continue in his role for some time, essentially devoting himself to his studies. Crautwald had a brief correspondence with Luther in 1526. Luther responded to Crautwald in an attempt to refute errors he detected in tracts Schwenkfeld had left in December 1525 (therefore elements of "spiritual feeding" were present before *Duodecium Questiones*). If Luther would write to Crautwald about a tract left by Schwenkfeld, this indicates that he knew that Crautwald was a co-religionist. Luther told Crautwald that he would wash his hands of him if he did not change his teaching on the Lord's Supper.

It is hard to say with any degree of accuracy what influence the Schwenkfelder had on the evangelische; however, Eberlein makes this contrast between the evangelische in Liegnitz and Wittenberg:

Wittenberger:	Liegnitzer:
God's action, objective holiness	Human experience, subjective holiness
Preaching law and gospel	Being made righteous (Mystik)
Word and sacrament	Spiritual baptism, inner revelation
A regional institutional Church	The community of believers
The ordained ministry	Priesthood of all believers[28]

27. Ibid., 28.

This list is helpful, but it is also suggestive of several things. For example, if one were to remove the statement on baptism, what is the difference between Eberlein's description of a "Liegnitzer" and a more generic, lay Pietism? Application of labels, especially by theological opponents, will be taken up when interpreting the events of 1708.

GOD'S FIREPLACE[29]

When a church visitation was made in one principality in 1558, four of the pastors were listed as Catholic, five as Schwenkfelder, and eight as Lutheran, a good indication that the best description one could give to the spirituality of the region is that the "situation was fluid."[30] It is to be noted that in the century following the Reformation, *Unitas Fratrum*, Schwenkfelder, Reformed, Lutheran, and Roman Catholic elements were present. Different areas of Silesia entered and exited the Reformation at different times as principalities reverted to Catholic rule. In reaction to the Counter-Reformation, "Barn-preaching" emerged, featuring repentance, prophetic visions, and apocalyptic prophesying, which helped fire a religious enthusiasm in the last decades of

28 "Wittenberger: Die Taten Gottes, das objective Heil; Die Gerechtsprechung des Sünders, extra nos am Kreuz; Die signa, Wort und Sakrament, Die Volkskirche, Die geordnete Predigtamt; Liegnitzer: Das menschliche Erlebnis, das subjektive Heil; Die Gerechtmachung des Sünders in Nobis (Mystik); Die Geisttaufe, die innere Offenbarung, Die Gemeinde der Gläubigen und Heiligen; Den Laiendienst, allgemeines Priestertum." Eberlein, Schlesische Kirchengeschichte, 50.

29. "Feuerherde Gottes," Ibid., 96. Helmut Eberlein uses the term when writing about the Pietists around the time of the Kinderbeten, but it applies further back.

30. Ibid., 58.

the sixteenth century called "storm clouds of Schwärmer and Inspired."[31]

However, it is not clear how many people were influenced by the Schwenkfelders. The Schwenkfelders at the time of the Kinderbeten were a small group, perhaps five hundred in all.[32] According to Horst Weigelt they were not introduced to radical Pietist ideas until the visit by the Petersens:

> As a result of these friendly contacts with Pietists, many Schwenkfelders began attending the services of pietis-tically-oriented pastors Johann Christian Schwedler of Nieder-Wiesa, Daniel Schneider in Goldberg and Johann Sturm . . . They allowed these men to perform marriages among them and to baptize their children.[33] They read Pietist writings (biographies rather than theological treaties)[34] continued to journey with their children to be baptized by Pastor Schwedler at Nieder-Wiesa.[35]

COUNTER-REFORMATION

Where the symbol of Reformation could be the Bible, the Hapsburg Counter-Reformation's could be a line they wanted people to cross over. Many of the more zealous persecutors were themselves converts to Catholicism. The Jesuits of that time were

---

31. *Bauern-predigern.* Eberlein mentions by name Antonius Oelsner, Christoph Oelsner, Martin John, and Michael Niedermeyer as *Bauernprediger* and Pastors Michael Hillerand as Erasmus Weichenhan as Schwenkfelder. *Inspierierten* means the Inspired. Ibid., 67.

32. Perhaps 500. See Weigelt, *The Schwenkfelders in Silesia*, 132.

33. Ibid, 118–9.

34. Ibid., 122.

35. Ibid., 132.

seen as "church-political-storm troopers."[36] Whereas Maximilian II was known for his comparative tolerance, his sons Rudolph II (ruled 1576–1611) and Matthias (ruled 1611–17) were "personal enemies of the Lutheran faith."[37] Each of the five emperors from the rule of Maximilian II to the war with Prussia in 1740 shared the same vision for re-Catholization. For example, Ferdinand II (ruled 1619–37) vowed three times to isolate the heretics.[38] The "church-reduction" policy was largely carried out in periods of especially harsh events in 1653–54, 1666, and 1668–1675. The death of Countess Elisabeth Lucretia in 1653 meant handing over Teschen to the Bohemian crown and the escalation of re-Catholization. Six hundred and fifty evangelische church buildings and property, along with the expulsion of the pastors and their families, occurred in 1653–64. Forty-nine buildings were taken in the Teshen area alone in 1654. The last of the Piasten royal line died in 1675, and more churches and schools were closed. Except for the three remaining Protestant principalities of Brieg, Liegnitz, and Oels and the city of Breslau, children were often forced to go to Catholic schools, families had to attend the Roman Catholic Mass and processions, and it became illegal to possess a Luther Bible and evangelische writings. In 1661 Leopold I, who ruled nearly fifty years until 1705, decreed that baptisms and other official ceremonies,[39] the reading aloud of

36. "Die kirchenpolitische Truppe, mit der Wiener Hof bei seiner Religions- und Kirchenpolitik unbedingt rechen konnte, waren die Jesuiten." Eberlein, *Schlesische Kirchengeschichte*, 71.

37. "Sie lebten schon in neukatholischer Frömmigkeit und waren persönliche Feinde des lutherischen Glaubens." Ibid.

38. Ibid.

39. *Kasualien* are baptisms, confirmation, marriages, and funerals. Previously, and in other periods and principalities, the evangelische clergy had to apply for permission and high fees had to be paid, which was a form of manipulation. With this decree, these necessary acts were forbidden so one needed to officially re-enter the Roman Catholic Church in order to be married, etc.

sermons, singing of church songs, and travel to border churches was forbidden. Church registers were to be handed over, and an indexing was done of remaining church property, for which a 10 percent tax was to be paid.[40] In Freystadt, thirty families with fifty-six children identified by Jesuits as evangelische were given three months to reconvert or their belongings would be sold.[41]

These efforts to reconvert were largely unsuccessful, shown in the flow of people into the Jesus Church in Teschen when they finally began construction of the church around 1720. The greater part remained true to the Reformation movement, aided by clandestine worship and secretly reading the Bible and evangelische literature. The focus shifted from parish church to family and small groups in the Counter-Reformation. They traveled on occasion to the forests and the mountains where they worshiped in fields and caves.[42] Another one hundred churches were confiscated as late as 1700. In total over twelve hundred churches were confiscated with their property, and their clergy with their families were expelled. It is little wonder that many Silesians saw Karl XII and his army as an answer to their prayers.

THE SPENER-FRANCKE CONNECTION

> In each spiritual movement which went through the German Church, Silesia had its share; so it remains that it was also not untouched by the movement of Pietism. The great men of German Pietism all became known in the lively religious circles in the Silesian Church. Spener, through his writings, A. H. Francke, through his rich correspondence and his many Silesian students at Halle, and Count Zinzendorf, through his personal travels and

40. Patzelt, *Pietismus in Teschen*, 22.
41. Patzelt, *Evangelischen Kirche in Österreichisch-Schlesien*, 34.
42. Ibid., 23.

> visits, and yes, Silesia stood next to his estate. As a result
> of such connections, revival fires flamed up here and
> there around the turn of the century in Silesia.[43]

Touched by many spiritual movements, impacted by the Reformation and the Counter-Reformation, Silesia was next influenced by the Spener-Francke movement. August Hermann Francke (1663–1727) was mentored by Phillip Jakob Spener (1635–1705), but whereas Spener had a vision to reform the Church, it is not an overstatement to say that Francke's vision was to change the world. It is said that Francke's mission was "universal regeneration." Much has been written by Silesian historians on Francke's connections with their homeland, his important friends and co-workers, the circle of pious Silesian nobles, the models of Halle Institute built in Silesia, and his involvement with the Altranstädter Convention.[44] "That Silesia had an important, strategic meaning for August Hermann Francke's world-wide reform plan has long been known."[45]

43. "An allen geistlichen Bewegungen, die durch die deutschen Kirchen gingen, hatte Schlesien seinen Anteil; so blieb es auch von der Bewegung des Pietismus nicht unberührt. Die großen Männer des deutchen Pietismus waren sämtlich den religious lebendigen Kreisen der schlesischen Kirche bekannt geworden. Spener durch seine Schrifften, A. H. Francke durch seinen reichen Briefwechsel und durch viele seiner Hallenser Schueler und Graf Zinzendorf, der ja räumlich Schlesien am nächsten stand, durch seine persönlich Reisen und Besuche. Infolge solcher Beziehungen flammte das Erweckungsfeuer von der Jahrhundertwende an hier und da in Schlesien auf." Eberlein, *Schlesische Kirchengeschichte*, 90.

44. See Wallman, *Der Pietismus,* 103–5 for a recent, comprehensive bibliography. Ward's "German Pietism, 1670–1750," 476–505, provides a helpful walk through the literature. See also Strom, "Problems and Promises of Pietism Research," 536–54.

45. "Das Schlesien fuer August Hermann Franckes weltweite Reformpläne eine strategisch wichtige Bedeutung hatte, ist für die Franckeforschung längst bekannt." Dietrich Meyer, „ Der Einfluß des

From early in his efforts at Halle, his Silesian "Circle of Nobles" was important, including the "Secret Counsel,"[46] that is, Count Heinrich XXIV von Reuß-Koestritz (1681–1748), Reichsgraf Erdmann Heinrich Henckel (1681–1752), and Erdmann II von Promnits-Sorau (1683–1745). The three had been students in Halle in 1698. They later built an orphan house, school, and Bible institute in Sagan in the principality of Sorau along the model of Halle.[47] In the introduction to the Pietist section of the source book on Silesian church history, Herbert Patzelt reported on the secretive alliance to promote the Lutheran Pietist cause in Silesia. Patzelt mentions Francke's friend and agent, Anhard Adelung, who wrote Francke from Teschen in 1709[48] about their new storefront whose warehouse would hide large amounts of Halle Bibles and tracts destined to be smuggled to Protestants in Hungary:[49]

> To this group, called the "secret council," also belonged
> Anhard Adelung, a member of the [Prussian] royal war
> council, a purchasing agent and missionary in Breslau,
> from 1706 to 1745 also political and church emissary

hallischen Pietismus auf Schlesien," Wallman und Sträter, eds. *Halle und Osteuropa: Zur europäischen Austrahlung des hallischen Pietismus*, 211.

46. "Geheimen Rat." "Secret Counsel" may seem a bit much until one considers the delicate Counter-Reformation political situation in their homeland and neighboring lands. Also, while Francke enjoyed a royal privilege for his school, the Prussian king did not desire a war with the Hapsburgs at that time. From Patzelt, "Introduction to Wirkungen des Pietismus in Schlesien," 159.

47. Schott, "Der Pietismus in Schlesien," 136. For a short, detailed examination of the Silesian nobles and all the various Halle models see Schwarz, "August Hermann Francke und Schlesien," *Jahrbuch für Schlesische Kirche und Kirchengeschicte,* 106–13.

48. Anhard Adelung to A. H. Francke, Teschen, 6.10.1709, StPk, Tüb., Kapsel 6, Bl.69 as in Patzelt, *Der Pietismus in Teschener Schlesien,*" 53.

49. ". . . hoffentlich den Karren aus dem Dreck heraus und über die Jablunker- und Karpathengebirge hinziehen werden"Anhard Adelung an Francke, Teschen, 7.7.1714, StPk, Tüb., Kapsel 27.

for Francke and man of confidence of Peter II of Russia. These religious and amicably connected men advised over the plans for the strengthening and bold propagation of the Lutheran faith life using their broad familial and personal connections, particular with the noble Silesians, both male and female).[50]

Francke's distinctiveness is seen in his activity, which was "according to his trust in God's provision with creative and urgent power."[51] He went personally to Altransträdt, using his connection with Count Reuß to lobby the Swedish king on the behalf of the Silesian Lutherans and religious freedom.[52] Perhaps the most important way Francke helped Silesia was in providing Bibles and edificatory literature. In the absence of a regular church community, for those living through religious oppression, the Bible, hymnbook, and edificatory literature such as tracts and Arndt's *True Christianity* took on extraordinary importance and became sources of new life. In the absence of a preacher,

50. "Zu dieser Gruppe, die sich "Geheimer Rat" nannte, gehörte auch Anhard Adelung, königlicher Kriegsrat in Breslau, Kaufmann und Missionar, von 1706 bis 1745 auch politischer und kirchlicher Abgesandter für Francke und Vertrauensmann Peters II. von Rußland. Diese glaubensmäßig und freundschlaftlich verbunden Männer berieten über die Pläne zur Festigung und Ausbreitung des lutherischen Glaubenslebens mit Hilfe ihrer weit verzweigten familiären und freundschaftlichen Verbindungen, insbesondere auch zu den adeligen Geschlechtern Schlesiens." *Quellenbuch zur Geschichte der evangelischen Kirche in Schlesien.*

51. ". . . der mit gestaltender und zwingender Kraft." Peschke, *August Hermann Francke, Studien zur Theologie*, 18.

52. "Francke war im Herbst 1706 persönlich in Altränstadt gewesen, der Hofprediger Karls XII. von Schweden im Winter desselben Jahres in Halle. Francke wie Graf Heinrich XXIV. bemuehte sich bei dem Schwedenkonig für die schlesischen Lutheraner und die Religionsfreiheit in Schlesien." Schwarz, "August Hermann Francke und Schlesien," 107.

these writings become a means of creating faith and "rose to the occasion," as it were. As Ward stated:

> Pietism might take a stricter line on things indifferent than Orthodoxy, but it did help to free the believer from Orthodox biblical literalism and opened men's eyes to a forgotten power in the original reformers . . . The Pietist rediscovery of the Bible as a means for creating and sustaining faith was not the same as the Reformed and Puritan habit of treating it as a book of precedents after the manner of the common lawyers.[53]

Johannes Wallmann's contribution to the recent fourth volume of Pietismus research, "Piety and Prayer," has an important observation concerning the Spener-Francke approach to prayer books. They did not use them! This is so simple it could go unnoticed. They relied so much on scripture and prayer and edificatory writing (tracts that taught on texts from scripture, stressed the importance of scripture, or were excerpts from scriptural sermons) that they had no need for prayer books. This was a break from the general use of prayer books. Though Luther had generally eschewed prayer books in favor of teaching people to view the Psalms as Christ's prayer book, a survey of publications show prayer books became quite popular in Lutheran Orthodoxy.

> In the half-century between the appearances of Spener's *Pia Desideria* 1675, the programmatic writing of Pietism, and Francke's death in 1726, truly few new prayer books appeared in the German book market. But their authors, e.g., Kaspar Neumann[54] and Benjamin Schmolck stood far from Pietism. None of the Pietists of the first genera-

53. Ward, "Review: Piety and Politics," 199–202.

54. Neumann was taken to task by Freylinghausen for his characterization of the Kinderbeten. Freylinghausen himself was the editor not of a prayer book but a hymnal.

tion, neither Spener, nor Francke or any of their circles
authored or published a prayer book.[55]

Last, what Francke and Halle gave to the evangelische in
Silesia was hope, a resource that is hard to measure empirically.
Francke's words, his repeated emphasis on trusting in God for
help in the battle against sin and darkness, encouraged Silesians
and reminded them of Spener's message of hope for better
times. Francke's deeds, particularly in providing education
and resources, showed he was someone who could be counted
on to provide more help. Francke and members of his circle
touched ancient cords. When revival broke out it was discerned
by Francke's co-worker and co-successor as "a spiritual break-
through wrought by God."[56]

THE SPIRITUALITY IMMEDIATELY PRECEDING
THE KINDERBETEN

One historian called Silesia "a religiously stormy land,"[57] and
another, "God's Fireplace."[58] Without a doubt, evangelische
Silesian nobles and some pastors and laity were part of the inner

55. "In dem halben Jahrhundert zwischen dem Erscheinen von
Speners Pia Desideria 1675, der Programmschrift des Pietismus,
und Franckes Tod 1726, erscheinen auf dem deutschen Buchmarkt
zwar vereinzelt noch neue Gebetsbücher. Ihre Verfasser – z.B. Kaspar
Neumann und Benjamin Schmolk – stehen aber dem Pietismus fern.
Keiner der Pietisten der ersten Generation, weder Spener noch Francke
oder einer aus ihrem Umkreis, hat ein Gebetsbuch verfasst oder zum
Druck gegeben." Wallman, "Frömmigkeit und Gebet," 83–101.

56. "Johann Anastasius Freylinghausen (1670–1739), Mitarbeiter
und Schwiegersohn, später auch Nachfolger Franckes, sah in der
Bewegung der betenden Kinder nicht in erster Linie eine Unordnung,
die möglichst bald beseitigt werden muss, sondern einen von Gott
gewirkten, geistlichen Aufbruch." Schott, "Pietismus in Schlesien," 139.

57. Conrads, *Altranstädter Konvention*, 69.

58. Eberlein, *Schlesische Kirchengeschichte*, 97.

circle of the Spener-Francke movement,[59] yet how much influence would Halle have had on the average Silesian, not to mention the average youngster in the Kinderbeten? One could assert that what Spener introduced in Germany as an additional measure to aid spiritual formation and effect discipleship was more like life support to the evangelische Silesians; however, a Pietist-like spirituality existed in Silesian homes before Spener was even born. "What Spener's *Pia Desideria* supported was long found in the practice of the people of Silesia, an inner prayer form."[60] They were "spiritual kindred,"[61] and even the Landeskirche evangelische overall had a predisposition to Pietism.

In the areas under re-Catholization the main concrete impact outsiders like Francke would have had was through the printed page: Bibles, hymnbooks, and tracts. Day in and day out they would be on their own. Evangelische believers worshiped in their individual homes, in house meetings with nearby believers, and in forest, mountain, and field clandestine services. Preachers would cross only infrequently from Saxony, Poland, and Hungary. It would be hard to say how often word and sacrament services would be held by the Silesian clergy who went into hiding in the *Gebirge*; perhaps funerals would bring them out. Silesians also journeyed to border churches to worship, traveling

59. See Patzelt, *Pietismus im Teschener Schlesien*; Stoeffler, *German Pietism During the Eighteenth Century*; Wallman, *Der Pietismus*; Ward, *The Protestant Evangelical Awakening*.

60. "Das, was Speners pia desideria forderte, fand sich in Schlesien unter dem Volke laengst in der Praxis geübt. Der Pietismus brachte daher fuer den Schlesier gleichsam die innere Bestaetigung und Anerkennung der eigenen Andachtsformen." Meyer, *Gnadenfrei*, 19.

61. "Wir dürfen die Bewegungen der betenden Kinder als eine Massenbewegung ansehen, die dem Pietismus verwandt ist und besonders das einfache Volk ihm erschliesst." (We should see the movement of the praying children as a mass movement, that is kindred spirit with Pietism and especially what the simple folk develop.) Ibid., 17.

long distances to hear sermons and worship in God's house.[62] A form of *Laienpietismus* emerged, not one that rejected clergy, but one that had to make do without. That and other hardships shaped their spirituality.

G. Meyer argued that Pastor Schwedler of Nieder-Wiesa, a *Grenzkirchen*,[63] had close connections with Francke and Halle and had opened an entrance for a revival movement. After all, Francke and Schwedler met as students in Leipzig in the 1680s, and they maintained a correspondence with Schwedler ordering printed materials from Halle to distribute and even beginning an orphanage. However, Schwedler was a Silesian, and the church he served was built in the 1650s by Silesians who received permission to build it across the river since it was illegal to build it in their community. While Halle helped, there was already a lay Protestantism in Silesia shaped by dependency on the Bible as the main source of finding a living faith that gets one through extreme spiritual hardship. The eager acceptance of Halle pietism was due to the fact that it resonated with what they already knew.[64]

The children of the Kinderbeten would have already had the simple prayer meeting form of Bible reading, hymn singing, and prayer modeled for them. When the oppressed Silesians would turn to the Bible for verses on prayer, one of the first to come to mind would be Matthew 18:19–20, which the 1545 Luther Bible has Jesus saying, "Where two will be on the earth, will I not be there? What they would ask my father in heaven will happen. I will be there with them where two or three gather in my name."[65]

---

62. Ibid.

63. "Border church." While border churches are an important feature of *evangelische* religious life in Lower Silesia until 1740 when the king of Prussia won Silesia and made evangelische worship legal again, Nieder-Wiesa seems to be unique in that it was built across the river by the evangelische in a town on the opposite side.

64. Meyer, *Gnadenfrei*, 17–19.

65. "Weiter sage ich euch: Wo zwei unter euch eins werden auf Erden,

A plain reading gives good reason to meet with a group to pray and expect to have prayers answered. One would also expect the living presence of Jesus. While it may be highly desirable to go to a church building and have a preacher, it is not necessary in order to have prayers answered.

The evangelische Silesians prayed for God to come to their aid and their expectation is seen in reading their letters. Theodor Wotschke collected and transcribed two collections of letters in 1929 and 1931. The following letter to Francke by Friedrich Opfergelt, a pastor in Oels, one of the Protestant principalities, in 1704, three years before the revival, reads:

> My prayer meetings which I have early on Sundays for one hour before going into the church, and one is held in my home in the evening at prayer time, has not been without noticeable blessings of God, but also not without allowing the greatest disgrace and persecution. God has himself already awakened his seed, wherefore with us, we heartily praise him.[66]

The following from *Gründliche Nachrichten* is an excerpt from one of the two collections of intercessory prayers reportedly overheard by the Kinderbeten:

---

warum es ist, das sie bitten wollen, das soll ihnen widerfahren von meinem Vater im Himmel. Denn wo zwei oder drei versammelt sind in meinem Namen, da bin ich mitten unter ihnen" (Matt 18:19–20).

66. "Meine Betstunden, die ich des Sonntags früh, eine Stunde zuvor, ehe man in die Kirche gehet, und auf den Abend, bei der Betglocke in meinem Hause halte, hat Gott nicht ohne merklichen Segen, aber auch nicht ohne die größeste Schmach und Verfolgung sein lassen. Gott hat sich schon einen seinen Samen erweckt, wovor ich ihm bitte mit uns herzlich zu preisen." Pastor Friedrich Opfergelt to A. H. Francke, 7 Februar 1704, Wotschke, "Urkunden zur Geschichte des Pietismus in Schlesien," *Jahrbuch des Vereins für Schlesische Kirchengeschichte*, 79–81.

> Dear God and Father, I have been wounded. How good it is to tell you, how much I am dust and ashes. Therefore, Lord, be not angry with me that I still speak more, but may the words of my mouth and the meditation of my heart be acceptable to you. You know, dear Father, that we together with still many thousands in our country and comrades in faith, the same as us, heartily request our places, which through your kindness we have presently received.[67]

Not appearing so very different than prayer meetings today around the world, they told their concerns and confessed their hope.

The evangelische also had the Small Catechism memorized, where it is taught:

> What does such baptizing with water signify? Answer: It signifies that the old Adam in us, together with all sins and evil lusts, should be drowned by daily sorrow and repentance and be put to death, and that the new man should come forth daily and rise up, cleansed and righteous, to live forever in God's presence.[68]

How might Luther's teaching have been especially suited to aid in this period of persecution? Luther's teaching simplified Christianity. For example, the above from the Small Catechism teaches something fairly complicated—realized eschatology (i.e.,

---

67. "Aber ach! O lieber GOtt und Vater/ ich habe mich unterwunden / mit dir zu reden/ wiewol ich Erde und Asche bin. Darum zürne nicht / HErrn/ daß ich noch mehr rede/ sondern laß dir wolgefallen die Rede meines Mundes/ und das Gespräch meines Hertzens fur die Dich. Du weist/ lieber Vater/ daß wir unsers Orts/ samt noch viel tausenden unsers gleichen/ das jenige auch hertzlich verlangen/ was unsere Lands=und Glaubens=Genossen durch deine Güte ietzund erhalten haben." *Gründliche Nachrichten*, 7.

68. Luther, *The Small Catechism*, in *The Book of Concord: The Confessions of the Evangelical Lutheran Church*, 349.

how God breaks into human existence)—in very simple terms. People could know that Jesus is with believers in their struggles. It is a simple, comforting, and empowering theology. A plain reception of "the old Adam in us, together with all sins and evil lusts, should be drowned by daily sorrow and repentance and be put to death, and that the new man should come forth daily and rise up, cleansed and righteous" means that one of the great conundrums of religion is solved. The baptized has a continuous, immediate source of divine connectivity and the future is not determined by fate or king or priest, only by God.

To summarize, Silesian spirituality centered on a much longed-for reform that had been in place since the late Middle Ages. With its appeal to *sola Scriptura* it represented a challenge to the ecclesiological structure of the dominant church, be it Catholic or Lutheran. This set the stage for the children's revival and the controversy to come between its supporters (Pietists) and the Lutheran clergy (Orthodoxy).

2

The Kinderbeten

*Particularly very good to observe in this matter and
to take the thing deep into the heart is that the prayer
of the children spread into five different principalities of the land of Silesia within approximately five
days. If at the same time a fast-moving wind storm,
a typhoon, developed and came on so fast and was
moved as by a hand, without a hidden divinity we
can not conceive such an impulse.*[1]

THE PREVIOUS chapter concerned an investigation of the
major elements comprising the Silesian religious context
but also cited the models that the children may have employed
for their prayer meetings—either that of the Swedish soldiers or
clandestine prayer meetings. This chapter attempts to do two
things: first, to reconstruct the historical event itself in terms of
its origin, what the children were in fact doing, and its relationship to the Swedish presence, and second, to investigate the

1. "Insonderheit ist dieses sehr wol zu beobachtet/ und in dieses
Sache tieff zu hertzen zu nehmen daß etwa innerhalb fünff Tagen in
fünff Fürstenthumern des Landes Schlesien das Gebet der Kinder nicht
anders als wenn ein geschwinder Sturm=Wind/ und Orcan entstanden/
zugleich und so geschwinde angegangen/ und sie mit gesammter Hand
dazu sind beweget worden / welches wir uns ohne einer verborgenen
Göttlichkeit/ so an den Trieb gegeben/ nicht concipiren können."
Petersen, *Die Macht der Kinder in der Letzen Zeit, auf Veranlassung Der
kleinen Prediger, oder, der betenden Kinder in Schlesien.*

interpretation of the event both by present and past historians in terms of their assessment of its divine origin, as well as the relationship of the revival with the clergy and the churches in the region. The controversy the revival reignited will be discussed in more detail in the chapter that follows.

THE CONTEXT OF THE REVIVAL

Silesia fared better after the Thirty Years War than its neighbors, Moravia and Bohemia. All were under the Hapsburg Crown, but whereas there were no or few allowances for the free expression of Protestantism in the latter two, three of Silesia's principalities retained some freedom of religion because of rights secured in the Treaty of Westphalia. All decisions concerning religion were bound by *cuius regio* and negotiations based on that policy were the means by which concessions or re-conversions were won. The three principalities of Oels, Liegnitz, and Brieg remained evangelische, and the main city of Breslau was permitted a few churches (minus steeple!) and a school. Since Silesia was 90 percent evangelische at the beginning of this period, many Silesians had few opportunities to exercise their religion. Into this situation marched the king of Sweden with four regiments. Earlier by letter and informal channels, then by direct appeal when he marched through in 1706 on his way to Poland from Saxony, Karl XII of Sweden had been made aware of the right granted at Westphalia for the king of Sweden to negotiate for the evangelische in Silesia in the case of treaty violations and was urged to exercise it. On his return march, Karl XII acted on this right. The Swedes' demands to return the evangelische churches were such that the chief Hapsburg diplomat, Count Wratislaw, wrote that he was negotiating with "wild men."[2]

The immediate larger political situation concerned the balance of power in Europe. They were in the midst of the War

2. Conrads, *Altranstädter Konvention*, 16.

of Spanish Succession (1701–14). Three Northern Protestant kingdoms, Hanover, Prussia, and Sweden, shared an understanding and were allied with England and Holland while the Austrian/Spanish Hapsburgs had their contest with the Bourbons over who was to be king of Spain. Emissaries from Portugal to Moscow, Naples to London were on high alert in the summer of 1707. Even the duke of Marlborough visited the camp of the Swedish king as they awaited the reply of Joseph I to the letter sent by his treaty negotiator, Count Wratislaw. It had appeared to the Hapsburgs that out of nowhere Karl XII was ready to go to war over securing a few articles of religious freedom in the relatively small land of Silesia. Although the Hapsburgs were fighting a war on four fronts and could hardly afford another with Sweden, who had recently defeated Prussia and Poland, this was still a very unusual and risky move by the Swedes.

Why did Karl XII risk so much? One story that circulated said he was there because on his march through Silesia on the way to Poland the year before, he had promised an old, gray-haired shoemaker in the town of Steinau that he would return and help the Silesian Protestants.[3] Would one of the most powerful monarchs in Europe risk the troops he needed for an impending war with a perennial enemy, the powerful czar of Russia, because he had given his word to a shoemaker? The story of the king and the shoemaker was no doubt part of the legend-building surrounding Karl XII at this time. When the gamble paid off and Joseph I made his concessions, Karl was lionized and spoken of as a second Gustavus Adolphus, his predecessor who, three-quarters of a century earlier, through courage and military and political genius, led the way to secure the continuation of the evangelische religion on the continent of Europe. Karl XII was also compared to Alexander the Great, another courageous, ambitious, young soldier-king. Commemorative medals were struck, songs were written, and his praises were published

3. Eberlein, "Die schlesischen Betekinder vom Jahre 1707/8.," 62.

as Protestant Europe claimed a new hero. Karl XII was compared in various printed sources to David and Solomon, having David's courage and Solomon's wisdom. Because of his decision to lose some churches and retain a nation, Joseph I was also compared with Solomon. That these events were interpreted as God acting on behalf of the evangelische Silesians is seen in the art of the frontispiece of publications with the details of the Altranstädter Convention (fig. 1).

The issues surrounding Karl XII's motivations in 1707 not only concern the "legend-building" dynamic but also intersect with the reasons behind the mass prayer meetings of the Silesian children.[4] Two motive questions are interrelated: why Karl marched into Silesia and why the children of Silesia began to hold prayer meetings. Accounts contemporary to the events and historians today say that an aspect of the first event, the children's witness of the Swedish soldiers worshiping in circular formation during morning and evening prayer, provided the inspiration of the second, the children's prayer meetings, which were also held outdoors in a circle, though some accounts at that time said imitation could not be the whole explanation. Historians should see these issues as being interrelated.

BET STUNDEN

Both the children's prayer meetings and the soldiers' morning and evening prayers are called *Bet Stunden.*[5] All other points

4. See Conrads, *Altranstädter Konvention*; Meyer, "Die Auswirkungen der Altranstädter Konvention auf die evangelische Kirche Schlesiens und die Bewegung der betenden Kinder," (chapter in book yet to be released, obtained from the author electronically, 9/11/2008).

5. Literally the term means "hour of prayer" and perhaps the best translation is "prayer meeting"; however, those terms already have specific meanings, therefore in the same manner the term evangelische is preferred to evangelical here because it can lead to confusion between Lutheran and a later more common usage, we keep the term *Bet*

aside, the Swedish soldiers' *Bet Stunden* must have been a sight to see. In 1621 Gustavus Adolphus established one of the first programs for military chaplaincy (*Militärkirchenordnung*), and his "war articles" lasted for two hundred years. Part of the military genius of the "Lion of the North," as Gustavus Adolphus was called, was to think through the inclusion of chaplains. The Swedes had morning and evening prayer daily, including while on maneuvers, and it seems they were very good at it. They accompanied chorale singing of the Psalms and hymns with trumpets and trombones while forming a circle on their parade ground. Lutheran hymnbooks still contain the liturgy for morning and evening prayer. They are the Protestant version of matins and vespers, part of the Catholic canonical hours of prayer.[6] After its opening verse, matins has a liturgical hymn of praise based on a psalm, a second psalm, a hymn, and one or two lessons from the Bible, a canticle based on a New Testament text, a collect, intercessions, the Lord's Prayer, the benediction, and another hymn. Seeing a choir of ten thousand men in their best uniforms must have been a stirring sight: "It was therefore a glimpse of the spiritual power of the army that the Silesians encountered."[7] The Swedish chaplains obviously intended to have some effect on the population, as they learned what tunes were used by the Silesians for the hymns they shared in common, but was all of this enough to spark a revival?

In the next section is a typical description of the form of the children's prayer meeting. Compare it to the description of the elements of the morning prayer service above. The children were also following an order similar to morning prayers. Nonetheless, this was not just done by the Swedish soldiers. The children

---

Stunden.

6. For example, the *Lutheran Book of Worship*, 131ff.

7. "Von daher läßt sich die auch geistliche Kraft der Armee erahnen, die den Schlesiern begegnete." Pawelitzki, "Das Schlesische Kinderbeten." In *Jahrbuch Schlesien Kirche Geschichte*, 91–100, here 94.

could know a very similar order from an informal prayer meeting. The children's meetings were reported to have begun in an area where evangelische worship was outlawed for fifty years. The children in this area must have participated in clandestine worship in homes or in the field or in the forest where a simple format of hymn singing, Bible-reading, and prayer was followed. Were the children following liturgical or prayer meeting style, or perhaps both?

GRÜNDLICHE NACHRICHTEN

In the Franckesche Stiftungen in Halle, Germany, one finds *Gründliche Nachrichten*, a long, thin book with an antique representation of the children at prayer (fig. 2). Included in its two-dozen pages are accounts of the activities, the judgments of Silesian clergy, and three lists of questions on the nature of the revival for the clergy to consider. The latter was probably written by interested laypeople who had a much more favorable interpretation of the events. Further research found these same exact contents in several other larger books, the most important being *Acta Publica,* which contains a few dozen publications concerning the Altranstädter Convention.[8]

Gründliche Nachrichten begins rather religio-philosophically[9] before transitioning into early modern religious journalism.

8. This work is found within the research of Norbert Conrads's *Die Durchführung der Altranstädter Konvention in Schlesien.* According to Dietrich Meyer, *Acta Publica* was prepared for the spring Frankfurt book fair, an impressive publishing feat, as it has dozens of reports and was completed within months of the events.

9. The first section of "Gründlichen Nachrichten," the collection of extracts of letters from Silesia, is approximately 3,131 words. The first 275 words serve as introduction before any of the historical facts enter in. It begins, "Daß der Zwang des Gewissens eine solche Sache und das jenige sey / was derer Menschen Gemüth/ja der Seele selbst am nähesten angehe/ dieselbe auch am allerhärtesten ein und empfindlichsten

The narrator/editor has incorporated extracts of letters being sent out of Silesia, along with tracts like "Fernere Nachricht" (A Further Report), which incorporates other material appearing in *Europa Fama* Part 74. The extracts read like a transcript of a mid-twentieth-century news announcer ("I've just been handed another report from Silesia"). The letters and reports concerning the events should be viewed as "eye-witness news" (i.e., accounts of what people thought they were seeing). They also include some discussion of how it was being interpreted by others. *Gründliche Nachrichten*'s author included *Gutachten*, the judgment of the ranking evangelische clergyman that the children were copying the soldiers, which Valentin Löscher passed on in *Unschuldige Nachrichten*.[10] Noteworthy is *Gründliche Nachrichten*'s opinion that many people questioned whether mimicry of the soldiers was all that was going on. *Gründliche Nachrichten* takes some pains to show it was weighing the reports from the Silesia carefully and shares with the writers of many of the other reports of the time that they knew what they were saying was important for future historians. Recitations of origin, methodology, and the obstacles encountered by the children from the authorities appear again and again in these accounts.

In a manner reminiscent of a newscast, a string of a dozen reports appear; this is not so strange considering much of *Gründliche Nachrichten* is taken from *Europa Fama*, which was a sort of an early newspaper. As noted above, the report contains the interesting item that the spread of the movement began on Holy Innocents Day. Christians who follow liturgical calendars in their worship still observe that day to acknowledge the dreadful slaughter by Herod in an attempt to kill the Messiah.[11] The

---

angreiffe/ist wohl ausser allem Zweiffel/und wird von keinem so leicht das Gegentheil zu behaupten seyn/massen denn auch Salomon davon saget : Ein ruhig Gewissen ist ein köstlich Gerüchte."

10. *UN*, 1709, 34–5.

11. This is an example of the type of historiography questions

historical narrative closes with two collections of prayers said to have been transcribed by adults listening to the children. The prayers sound much like one might hear at a prayer meeting today—asking for forgiveness, that the word of God might be better known, that God would send his Holy Spirit on the people, that God would send revival, that God would show favor on them, and that they might become messengers for God.

SIMILARITIES IN THE SILESIAN REPORTS

The awakening began in the mountains, creating a sensation as it spread, giving birth to numerous eyewitness accounts bearing remarkable similarity. A dozen of these "extracts" appear in *Gründliche Nachrichten* and appear below in translation with the material common to each conflated for the following:

> It had begun in the Silesian mountains and thereafter gone forth from one place to another. By it the children show such an uncommon reverence and zeal that neither their parents nor anyone else are able to hold them away. Sometime after Christmas, around December 28, Holy Innocents Day, it began spreading through Silesia reaching five provinces in five days. The children, male and female, four to fourteen years in age, with an unusual devotion for their age, assemble themselves in a certain place to pray together with childlike devotion daily. They come together in the morning about seven, around noon, and around four [it was winter]. These

addressed later in the chapter. This and other explanations for the supernatural may raise eyebrows or elicit chuckles from historians today. However, one can be thrown off track in learning what questions should be asked by other easily answered aspects of the whole situation. That is, skepticism about one element (Holy Innocents Day) and skepticism of supernatural causation in general does not mean that a more plausible explanation, that religious people are inspired by hope, should be overlooked.

poor, hard-pressed children, out of their own desire and without their being given some prescribed method, began to assemble to pray. Indeed, without any direction from any adult, not only were they not given help, but were even having to act against the commands of the religious and civil authorities, and against their parents, who made threats and laid hindrances in their way. The children initiated this within their villages, towns, and cities; however, when their gatherings were not tolerated, they chose to keep to themselves [outside the city] in open fields and under the open sky. They hold orderly prayer meetings, singing, reading the Bible; they fall on their knees, and at some places it is reported they fall on their faces praying and repenting. It had begun sparse but in many places it grew to three to four thousand people. The places have crowds of people coming to regard the unusual devotion of the tender children. The children kneel on the ground almost the whole time of the prayer meeting. They have chosen from their midst a reader for this purpose who a stands in the middle, reads aloud, and leads not only the songs but also the prayers, which are clearly audible from a distance. [One fairly typical but more detailed description stated] Ordinarily they sing seven songs, and a prayer comes between each one; they have a psalm of repentance, and they read a chapter from the Bible; in the end the children lift hands together upward and sing [two more hymns]. The bystanders cannot regard it without being moved to tears hearing the prayers. Truly, one can hear the singing nearly a quarter mile away. They have among their prayers also one which is to ask that dear God give their churches back to them. No one knows how the children would have gotten such a longing without the parents' knowledge.[12]

The discontinuities in the reports include whether they used prayer books, if they met in churches, and a few inclusions

12. *Gründliche Nachrichten*, Translated by the author.

of the names of adults who were seen watching. In other words, the reports are remarkable for their similarity. It seems the children had no fixed rule as to using prayer books, as two reports speak of the use of prayer books. "After they have sung their Hymns, they read some Prayers out of John Arndt, his Garden of Paradise . . ."[13] One report from Breslau says, "They pray the most beautiful prayers out of their little books." Another report said the Swedish negotiator, von Strahlenheim, witnessed the revival. One extract notes that one of the Silesian nobles mentioned in chapter 1 was seen worshiping while looking on. That report is one of the few that give any interaction between the children and the adult bystanders. The youngster there was apparently acting as an evangelist and was reported to have said that if they wanted to change from their sins, God would be merciful to them and would absolve them. Other discontinuities are a few incidents of a supernatural nature, but there are only a few, which is in keeping with the author's stated purpose of attempting to present a factual report.

PROVIDENTIAL

Most of the allusions to the supernatural in *Gründliche Nachrichten* are confined to opinions about the revival's origin and progress. As is the case with documents of the period it is commonplace to state that God is the mover of a situation. For example, these events were interpreted as God acting on behalf of the evangelische Silesians, which is seen in the art of the frontispiece of publications with the details of the Altranstädter Convention (fig. 1).

A few supernatural occurrences were reported. The children showed no reaction when a cavalry troop pretended to charge at them. Many adults, even "the roughest," were led to tears. This is a fairly common element in accounts of other reviv-

d13. "Praise Out of the Mouth of Babes," 13.

als, yet we see here that it was not the result of fiery preaching but being in the presence of the quiet worship of children. However, a miraculous element is given in the last extract: the letters of the prayer books began to irradiate light and doves were flying around the children close enough to touch. (This obviously irked some of the Silesian Orthodox Lutheran clergy, as one wrote, "So let us hear no more about birds.") A *nota bene* at the end of the reports in *Gründliche Nachrichten* states that there were many other reports that could have been included that contained other "occurrences," but he held them back as they were being printed elsewhere. It is reasonable to assume that its intent was to keep distance from charges of dubiousness, as it stated at the beginning of the reports, "Nothing less than sound truth will be encountered herein." One should note that there are more of these supernatural incidents in the English language publication *Praise out of the Mouth of Babes* than in the German reports. In the latter the main providential aspect of the revival in Silesia is the changed nature of the children, how previously wild and mischievous youngsters who would have to be drug to church now could not be held away from praying.

PRAISE OUT OF THE MOUTH OF BABES

One discrepancy between the English language version and the German reports is the former mentions the Swedish soldiers only once and downplays their influence: "It may be that the Rise therof was taken from the Hours of Prayer, observed by the Swedish Soldiers quartered there last Autumn."[14] Dowling's version has a preface by Josiah Woodward, something the English reformer of manners wrote in 1706 concerning revival, that indicates the manner in which the English evangelicals interpreted the news of the Kinderbeten (i.e., it was something they were looking for). It is followed by "Recommendation of

14. Ibid., 4.

another Eminent Divine of the Church of England." This refers to the king of Prussia, which indicates that the English friends of Halle saw the revival related to the work of A. H. Francke. Before the actual narrative begins, there is another unsigned "To the Reader," which was probably written by A. W. Boehm in collaboration with Count Ludolph. Francke sent Boehm, one of his earliest and most trusted graduates, to London some years previously. Count Ludolph was secretary to Prince George of Denmark, the husband of Queen Anne. Ludolph had spent time at Halle, was a confidant of Francke, and like Anhard Adelung, was also a confidant of Czar Peter. Boehm had become chaplain to Prince George as well as secretary to Society for Promoting Christian Knowledge (SPCK).

Boehm collated Ludolf's diaries and journals into *Reliquiæ Ludolfianæ,* which concludes with the eulogy he gave at a funeral attended by the members of SPCK.[15] The library at the Stiftungen has a handwritten manuscript appearing to be a copy book of Ludolf's, which has material similar to *Praise out of the Mouths of Babes* but is much shorter. The handwritten book begins:

> Extract of a credible account received out of Silesia concerning the Children there in there dayly assemble to worship God. Allmost all the children in the Nether Silesia in most parts are enkindled with a deep reverence to glorify God. There is scarce a village in Lignizwhere they go—[16]every day assemble in the open air in the

15. Ludolf and Böhm, *Reliquiæ Ludolfianæ: the pious remains of Mr. Hen. Will. Ludolf; consisting of I. Meditations upon retirement from the world. II. Also upon divers subjects tending to promote the inward life of faith, &c. III. Considerations on the interest of the church universal. IV. A proposal for promoting the cause of religion in the churches of the Levant. V. Reflections on the present state of the Christian church. VI. A homily of Macarius, &c. To which is added, his funeral sermon, preach'd by Anthony William Boehm, chaplain to His late Royal Highness Prince George of Denmark.*

16. The word looks like "nue." Also, the word "*retiredriste*" is a best

> greatest tranquillity and deepest introversion of mind
> and *retiredriste*, to hold hours for praying which is also
> practiced upon the mountains and other places. Some of
> the ministers do behold and wink at this practice, others
> rage against it, and very few are pleased to see it.[17]

No attributions were given, but it includes excerpts from
the letter of Pastor Schindler from Liegnitz, and like *Praise out of
the Mouths of Babes*, it has material from both *Europa Fama* and
Gründliche Nachrichten.

Halle's connection to London and New England's connection through the Mathers are well documented.[18] Increase Mather
(1639–1723) also released a copy of *Praise out of the Mouths of
Babes* in June 1709.[19] Mather's introduction indicates that news
of the Kinderbeten raised the hopes of far-flung Protestants and
was seen as an apocalyptic sign:

> The Narrative Emitted herewith, having been sent to me
> from London, I was willing that people in these remote
> American parts of the Earth should be acquainted with
> it, and have therefore committed it to the Printer in order
> to its being here Published. The History is Confirmed
> by so many Letters from Credible Persons, that there
> seems no room left to Question the Truth of what is

attempt at transcription.

17. AFSt/HD23b 15–6, Eintrag Einzelstück, Schreiben von Heinrich
Wilhelm Ludolf an Abendanon (Abschrift). The quote here is as exact a
transcription as possible; the use of "sic" has been avoided.

18. Brunner, *Halle Pietists in England: Anthony William Boehm
and the Society for Promoting Christian Knowledge*; Sames, *Anton
Wilhelm Bohme (1673–1722): Studien zum okumenischen Denken und
Handeln eines halleschen Pietisten*; Lovelace, *The American Pietism
of Cotton Mather: Origins of American Evangelicalism*. Ward's works
contain a wealth of information about these connections; see also
Benz, "Ecumenical Relations between Boston Puritanism and German
Pietism: Cotton Mather and August Hermann Francke," 159–93.

19. See note 13, Introduction.

related. Concerning the design of Providence in such a strange Dispensation I shall say nothing. *Deus et dies docebunt*. We must leave it to GOD and Time to make the Discovery. Only this in Conjunction with several other things lately happening, which are wonderful and unaccountable, give us just ground to expect that great Changes are near unto the World.[20]

The tract itself is made up of four sections, credits *Europa Fama,* but also has material from *Gründliche Nachrichten* as well as another so-far unidentified source and closes with the final words of Neumann's *Gutachten.* The second section contains some reports not found in any of the German resources examined. One reports the children being "fired on without ball," but they were not frightened at the least. Section Four gives the twenty-one reasons from *Europa Fama* why the revival should be seen "as good and from God" which concludes with advice on how to receive revivals:

> The Conclusion is: That where-ever these Characters, or at the least the chief and strongest of them are found, *the thing must be judged Good and Divine*, at least so long as nothing appears to the contrary. Neither doth it follow, that, if perhaps some Irregularities in Tract of Time should mingle with these Spiritual Operations; therefore the first motion is not of God neither: It happens too often, and that even to Aged People, *that they begin in the Spirit and end in the Flesh*. Nor would it be a Prejudice to these Characters, if in some Places, Faults and Disorders should creep in among 'em. Or do we think it will hold, to say: that there is nothing of God in a matter subject to some Imperfections. Nor doth it follow, that a thing must be bad, because some Clergymen disapprove of it: for it must be inquired into whether they have sufficient Reason for it. When the

20. Ibid.

> Children cried in the Temple, and said *Hosanna*, the
> Priests and Scribes *were sore displeased,* Matth. 21.15.
> And nevertheless the Lord looked upon it, as the fulfill-
> ing of Scripture. Prudence must be used in this affair,
> that on the one hand by untimely Commendation, the
> Children might not be inspired with a secret Pride on
> Account of their Devotion; and on the other Hand, their
> Mistakes be so mildly corrected, that the good Motions
> not be rooted out, nor their Love to Prayers quenched.
> In short: if the children do not perform it well and godly
> enough, and faults are discovered in their Prayers, the
> old ones may look to themselves, and see to do better;
> that so they may set a more complete Pattern before
> their Eyes, & so really teach 'em, that one ought not trifle
> with the great Concern of Religion.[21]

Thus we have seen that accounts of the revival in Silesia
were published on the continent, England, and the colony at
Massachusetts through early experiments in journalism, as well
as in books. The children's movement was viewed in providential
terms and in an entirely positive way in the English translations.
It is to be observed that negative comments came from the clergy
of Lutheran Orthodoxy, while the Pietists and Evangelicals were
positive. The above report was published first in Massachusetts
in 1709 a few decades before the Great Awakening in the
colonies but was republished in 1741. This could be due to interest in making sense of what they had experienced by looking
at similar events in the past. Both *Praise out of the Mouths of
Babes* and Jonathan Edwards' (1703–58) *A Faithful Narrative of
the Surprising Work of God* state that the revivals were providential. Johann Adam Steinmetz, who was senior pastor of the Jesus
Church at Teschen, translated Edwards' *A Faithful Narrative of
the Surprising Work of God,* which is an endorsement of sorts that

21. Ibid., 21.

the two revivals were similar from the point of view of someone who had been through it a few decades earlier.

Historians point to Wesley's experience at Aldersgate as determinative, but it should be noted that while he received a "warmed heart" and the longed-for "joy in the Holy Ghost," it was gone in a few days. When did Wesley cease writing in his journal about his nagging doubts (besides the odd reference here and there throughout his life)? He did so after reading Edwards's *A Faithful Narrative of the Surprising Work of God*. We see the same effect from the relation between hope and prayer as we see in Silesia (i.e., "If God did that, what might else He do, and for me?").

WHAT CAN HISTORIANS SAY ABOUT THE KINDERBETEN?

We address now the two possibilities given on the doubt of origins, and as stated, these might be resolved by the references to prayer. In 1899 Gerhard Eberlein, then dean of Silesian church historians, posed some interesting historical questions in "Die Schlesischen Betekinder vom Jahre 1707/8."[22] There he was most interested in what could be learned about the origin of the Kinderbeten, but this does not even figure in more current histories. This itself is an interesting historical question. Eberlein wrote that while we no longer need nor want to worry our heads over whether the revival was a work of the devil, from God, or had mixed influences, the most urgent question was when and where did it begin.[23] While current historians would be

---

22. Eberlein, "Die schlesischen Betekinder vom Jahre 1707/8," 52.

23. "Gewiß werden wir uns nicht mehr den Kopf zu zerbrechen brauchen oder nur wollen, ob hier ein Teufelswerk oder ein goettliche Sache oder gar ein „gemischter Fall" vorliegt. Aber gerade über das, was wir vor allem wissen möchten, weil es zur Beurteilung dringend nötig ist, wann und wo die Andacht ihren Anfang genommen hat, lassen uns alle jene „Nachrichten" und „Prüfung" trotz der „Gründlichkeit", die sie

inclined to view a beginning date of Holy Innocents Day for a revival led by children skeptically, is there really no interest in its "origin and sources"? We are, of course, interested in what past historians said about where the revival came from, and it seems that scholars should still be interested in how it originated. As stated before, historians today assume they must be scrupulously skeptical. Is this why the reason of the children imitating the soldiers is passed on?

Eberlein wrote bluntly, "The message that one can sometimes read until present-day, that in Sprottau the Kinderbeten had taken its beginning is false."[24] His evidence is a report that said, "Many thousand knew" that the children prayed through the whole summer in 1707 in the mountains and at several places of the Glogau principality.[25] His article should be required reading for anyone interested in the Kinderbeten, yet it only made the footnotes in one recent article with no discussion in the article itself, and when interviewed, the author had no question that

wenigstens auf dem Titel haben im Ungewissen." Ibid.

24. "Die Nachricht, die man bis heutigen Tages manchmal lesen kann, daß in Sprottau das Kinderbeten seinen Anfang genommen habe, ist falsch." Ibid.

25. "Dagegen ist sicher, daß die zuverlässigsten Nachrichten nach dem Riesenbirge weisen als der Gegend, wo die Sache begonnen habe. „Viel tausend wissen", daß 1707 fast den ganzen Sommer durch die Kinder im Gebirge und an etlichen Orten des Glogau'schen Fürstentums gebetet haben." Ibid. Eberleins reference is „Zur Geschichte des Pietismus in Schlesien von 1707–1740, Von Dr. C. A. Schmmelpfennig, ev. Pfarrer in Arnsdorf." *In Zeitschrift des Vereins* für *Geschichte und Alterthum Schlesiens.* Namens des Vereins herausgegeben von Dr. Colmar Gruenhagen. Breslau, Joseph Mar and Komp,1868. The source is identified by Schmmelpfennig as Caspar Neumann: "Nach Caspar Neumann hingegen „ist fast den ganzen Sommer 1707 durch die Kinder im Gebirge, auch an etlichen Orten im Glogauschen Fürstenthum schon gebetet worden." "Following Caspar Neumann on the other hand, "Almost throughout the summer of 1707 the children have prayed in the mountains, also at several places in Glogau principality."

the origin of the revival was that the Silesian children copied the Swedish soldiers.[26]

Other recent accounts (Ward, Schott, Patzelt, Schmitt, etc.) give imitation of the Swedish soldiers as a matter of course, as do authors of some of the original round of reports. However, while some of the older accounts, especially the ones by the Pietists, grant that the Swedes might have been the original inspiration, they also assert that there was something else going on that was seen in observing the unusual and lasting devotion of the children. A few, like Freylinghausen and Petersen, asked directly, as G. Eberlein did two centuries later, why the children in Saxony, where the Swedes were a whole year previously, did not also copy them, but no one before or since Eberlein gave much importance to the reports of activity in the mountains. Dietrich Meyer is the only contemporary historian to have investigated these 1708 accounts in his published work. Why do most of the historians pass on Neumann's story that the children were inspired by the sight of the Swedish soldiers and not see that there was another model they may have been using, the form of the clandestine prayer meeting? Why does no one ask why Neumann knew that the children had been praying before the arrival of the Swedes yet said they were imitating the soldiers?

The best insight to determining when and where would be to ask the how. How was all over the original reports; even Neumann said it was from God. God caused it. That may be, but it is no answer to satisfy a historian, and many would not even consider it an interesting question. However, ask a Lutheran theologian and one might well hear, "God did it through a proclamation of the word," and with that information a historian could take another look at the evidence. The Silesians had been told to hope and pray that God would hear their cry and come to their aid, so they prayed. If "many thousands knew" that these children's prayer meetings were going on for months before the

26. Interview with Pia Schmid, June, 2008.

surprise visit of the Swedes, the reasonable thing would be to look for evidence in the upper Silesian record of sermons and testimonies in the period between 1647 and 1707. Admittedly, that is not easy to do. Still, considering that the children's prayer meetings originated in the area that had seen the harshest repression of religious freedom and evangelische worship could only be held clandestinely, the next question would be what was the form of that worship? If what the children were doing did look like morning prayer but it was even closer to the kind of prayer meetings held by people around the world, is it not reasonable to call into question the theory that the children were imitating the soldiers? In the accounts of the period no one suggested that the children were imitating their parents. Orthodoxy and Pietists both attributed the origin to the children's imitation of the Swedes, with the latter suggesting that this was not all that was going on, alluding to providence there as well, and contemporary accounts point only to the imitation of the soldiers.

Ironically, the Swedish soldiers did inspire an imitation. It is reasonable to assume that people had prayed for peace and religious freedom and when the Swedish soldiers showed up they took this as a sign that God was answering their prayers. It is also reasonable to assume that testimony concerning answered prayer would inspire hope that other prayers might be answered among those who believed that God answers prayer. If we return to figures 1 and 2, we can now see that there is more than meets the eye. The second resembles the first, and in one sense, it can be said that it "was inspired by it," as in "the artist copied it." It was reported then and still today that the children in the second picture were copying the Swedish soldiers. Perhaps it can or should be said that the second scene, the revival, was inspired by the Swedish soldiers because they embodied a divine answer to the prayer for political liberation in the minds of the Silesians, but this refers to the larger revival that was reported to have spread after Christmas 1707. The earlier prayer movement in the

Gebirge still needs to be explained, and the children knowing how their parents prayed and for what they had prayed is the only possible explanation. Perhaps the most curious thing about this most curious revival is that no one then or now seems to have thought this worth comment.

The following chapter begins with a lengthy close reading of *Prüfung*, whose purpose is to get inside the theology of the Pietist movement led by Francke. After that, we look at *Die Macht der Kinder* to learn more what a more radical Pietist theologian thought as he searched scripture, heavens, and voices from far countries.

3

Pietist and Lutheran Orthodox

Reactions to the Revival

THIS CHAPTER dealing with historical-theological reflections begins with profiles of the authors of the works under
discussion, *Gutachten, Prüfung,* and *Die Macht der Kinder.*
Gutachten is a report given on the children's revival by the chief
evangelische pastor in Silesia, Caspar Neumann, inspector of the
church and school in Breslau. *Prüfung* is the somewhat vitriolic
(or perhaps exasperated is a better word) response of Johann
Anastasius Freylinghausen, an example of Pietist thinking in the
vein of Spener-Francke pietism. This is followed by *Die Macht
der Kinder* by Johann Wilhelm Petersen, an example of the
thinking of someone labeled a radical Pietist.

It will be argued that mainstream and radical Pietists both
saw the revival as a work of God and attempted to place it within
the broader framework of salvation history over what they
perceived was a lukewarm reception by Lutheran Orthodoxy.
Due to their chiliasm and apocalypticism, Pietists saw the
history of salvation in terms of continuous divine intervention.
This fueled their prayer meetings and led them to see the prayer
revival as a sign of God's ongoing renewal of the church in antici-
pation of the end of all things.

CASPAR NEUMANN, J. A. FREYLINGHAUSEN, AND J. W. PETERSEN

Pastor M. David Schindlers wrote that many of the clergy in Silesia "raged against" the revival. What happened to the Silesian evangelische spirituality following the Reformation that Schott said was so warm-hearted? Is it reasonable to surmise that this was a consequence of the Counter-Reformation? In having to define themselves against Roman Catholicism, did the evangelische become very much like the Lutheranism of Valentin Löscher? This was a time of Lutheran Orthodoxy constantly defining itself against Roman Catholics, Anabaptists, Enthusiasts, Reformed, Socinianists, and Pietists. It seems strange to admit something is from God but then set about immediately to alter it significantly. One wonders if constant dogmatic warfare makes for party spirit, or is it simply exceedingly cautious of anything new and thus unable to see real value and make allowances?

Six weeks into the revival, Caspar Neumann (1648–1715) gave a report on it during the sermon in his congregation's evening prayer. It was printed under the title *Unvorgreifflichen Gutachten* or "A Humble Credible (or 'Expert') Account." It became part of each collection of reports being printed and circulated in Europe concerning this strange revival. Neumann gave a mixed review of the revival. Although some Pietists and their friends were disappointed or even outraged at some of the things he wrote, they continued to refer to *Gutachten* because of Neumann's status as an authority coupled with his assessment that the revival was of divine origin and should not be forbidden. However, as Neumann himself said, he did not understand it, and it is doubtful whether what he said added much clarity to the overall understanding of the revival. His mixed review provided fodder for both Pietists and the Orthodox. Who was Caspar Neumann?

Besides being an evangelical clergyman Neumann was an educator and scholar. He was a pioneer in applying strict observations of human life in developing scientific principles, and the methodology he used in compiling the population statistics of Breslau occasioned Gottfried Leibniz (1646–1716) to send his work to the Royal Society of London. He was made a member of the Berlin Academy of Sciences in 1706. Should Neumann be seen as a *Frühaufklärung* figure who is ambivalent toward the supernatural? Coupled with the usual fear Lutheran clergy had that an Enthusiast might create an uproar in his community, we have someone who could acknowledge that the revival was from God yet treat it with mild contempt. But should his report be viewed as a scientist placing the children under a microscope and not knowing exactly what was being observed?

Neumann is an interesting figure worthy of additional research. He was not a Pietist, though one of his biographers said he had a warm-hearted piety and was a Pietist of sorts.[1] Early as a Lutheran cleric he had been chaplain to a son of Duke Ernst the Pious. He is known for his hymnal, *Vollkommenes Schlesisches Kirchengesangbuch* (1703), which enjoyed a long popularity in Silesia, and prayer book, *Kern aller Gebete*, which went through dozens of editions.[2] That alone would suggest that his sensibilities struck a deep note with his compatriots. In regard to his thoughts on Pietism and relationships with Pietists, we know that he made the trip to Halle, toured the *Waisenhaus,* and said some good things about Francke's work, but when it came to his own territory, he was much tougher on Pietists. Ward wrote that Neumann had done much to undermine the devotional and intellectual attitudes of the old Orthodoxy,[3] but the *Gutachten*

1. See Zimmerman. "Caspar Neumann und die Enstehung der Frühaufklärung."

2. See Schott, "Caspar Neumans ‚Kern Aller Gebete' Zum 350. Geburtstag des Breslauer Kircheninspektors," 243–51.

3. Ward, *Protestant Evangelical Awakening,* 73.

shows when it came to anything approaching a resemblance to Enthusiasm, he shared the view of Lutheran Orthodoxy. We know by his words, "There is no vice in piety but there is in Pietists,"[4] as well as what he wrote in *Gutachten*, that he was not a member of the Pietist party. He seemed to be scandalized by the notion of prayer in the streets. However, one factor not considered yet is the political situation.

Caspar Neumann was the leader of the Lutherans in the capital of Silesia. As such, he knew Hapsburg authorities well. Part of his negative reaction to the large public prayer meetings that drew as many adult onlookers as the children participating was surely concern that the authorities would either discern a threat of rebellion or that it would be used as a pretext to clamp down and reverse recent gains in religious freedom or worse. In other words, Neumann might have acted to bring the children's prayer inside the church not because he was scandalized by the idea of public prayer but in order to not antagonize the Hapsburgs.

Neumann had told parents and authorities that the children should not be kept from continuing their prayer. One of the *Gründliche Nachricht* extracts from Breslau shows that in March he had already implemented his plan to use two recently returned churches and place the praying children under clergy who would lead their prayers. Considering the issue of freedom of religion, it is ironic that he was able to do this because a number of the confiscated church buildings in Breslau were returned to the *evangelische*, but the revival in which the children had prayed for the return of their churches then ran out of steam.

Johann Anastasius Freylinghausen (1670–1739) was A. H. Francke's co-worker (*Mitarbeiter*) at Halle. Freylinghausen matriculated at the University of Halle in 1692 and became adjunct at St. George Church, the congregation of which Francke was senior, in 1695. When Francke was named pastor at Halle's main church, St. Ulrich's, Freylinghausen was also made one of its two pastors. In

4. *non vitium pietas, sed pietismus habet.* Ibid.

1723 he was named sub-director of the institutes at Halle, and following Francke's death in 1727, he became co-director along with Francke's son, Gotthilf August Francke. Freylinghausen's main work was his *Geistreiches Gesangsbuch*, first published in 1706. He wrote forty-four hymns. It would be hard to find a person more self-identified with the movement begun by A. H. Francke. Therefore, in the absence of a record of A. H. Francke's opinion on a given matter, something by Freylinghausen is close. Freylinghausen's *Lebenslauf* corroborates Löscher's supposition in *Unschuldige Nachrichten* (1709) that Freylinghausen was the author of *Prüfung*, an anonymous tract that takes to task Caspar Neumann's *Gutachten*.

Johann Wilhelm Petersen (1649–1727) matriculated in theology and philosophy at the University of Gießen, was adjunct in philosophy in Rostock, then professor of poetry, was pastor in Hanover in 1677, and was superintendent and Hofprediger in Eutin in 1678. In 1686 he returned to Rostock as doctor of theology. In 1688 became superintendent in Lüneburg, and in 1692 he was deposed on account of *Schwärmertum* (his radical chiliastic teaching). The Petersens were both members of Spener's early Frankfurt *collegio*. Petersen's wife, Johanna Eleonora née von Merlau (1644–1724), moved there in 1675 in order to participate in it. A noble lady, her marriage to a commoner occasioned a minor scandal at the time, and she received more notoriety for her publications in the late 1680s, in which she wrote of her visions. She and her husband published extensively. After his deposition, a pious advisor to the king of Prussia helped him to buy an estate that had been out of use since the Thirty Years War, and the Petersens devoted themselves to writing and discerning the signs of the times. Petersen took Spener's ideas concerning *chiliasmus* to their logical and prophetic conclusions. Naturally, *Die Macht der Kinder* is an apt vehicle for this. In-depth study of this book and Petersen's overall theological contribution still remains to be done.

Die Macht der Kinder is suitable to the purpose at hand because not only is it a judgment on the revival by a doctor of theology, who, deposed or not, did solid work, but Petersen also returns again and again to the events and their written reports. He, in fact, weaves them into his book (whose full title in English is *The Power of the Children in the End Time, on Account of the Cause of the Little Preachers, or the Praying Children in Silesia*). [5]

With the succinct words, "My dear husband was called to Silesia to get to know about the praying children . . ." the historian learns from Petersen's equally famous wife that he not only traveled to Silesia and saw the awakening firsthand, but also that he was asked to come (who asked him is unknown, but it would be reasonable to assume that it was one of the circle of the pious nobles).[6] The above is from a letter referred to in a recent biography[7] in which one searches in vain for a pronouncement of her judgment of the revival. Her husband's book, on the other hand, gives copious judgments. By entitling his report *Die Macht der Kinder*, Petersen spoke loud and clear concerning God's power and purpose in the children's prayers. Specifically, he said the praying children were a sign from God that the day of the Lord was at hand. He saw many things in it; one of the hopeful things was that God was giving the world another chance.

---

5. *Die Macht der Kinder in der Letzen Zeit, auf Veranlassung Der kleinen Prediger/ oder/ der betenden Kinder in Schlesien/ Aus der Heiligen Schrifft vorgestellet von Johann Wilhelm Petersen, der H. Schrifft D. The Power of theCchildren in the Last Time, at the Request of the Small Preachers, Prayer or the Children in Silesia, from the Holy Schrifft presented by Johann Wilhelm Petersen, PhD.*

6. "Mein lieber Mann war nach der Schlesie beruffen/ um das Kinder=Gebeth mit anzuhören." AFSt 65G2.

7. Petersen, *The Life of Lady Johanna Eleonora Petersen, Written by Herself.*

PRÜFUNG

A few more words about *Gutachten* and *Prüfung* are in order before we examine them.[8] *Gutachten* was given by Neumann at the time of the sermon in a mid-week, evening worship service and is sermon-length. All of *Gutachten* is included in *Prüfung,* as it is used in its entirety as a skeleton for Freylinghausen to hang his theological reflections on. Therefore, any review of *Prüfung* includes discussion of *Gutachten.*[9]

Freylinghausen's criticisms center around three areas:

1) Neumann's methodological approach to the revival;

2) Neumann's use of pejorative terms that implicitly call the revival into question;

3) Neumann's failure to focus on the source.

His opening words are a foretaste of the tart judgments to come: "It is an examination of the so-called humble, credible account,[10] but no one should be encumbered by the idea that Neumann's *Gutachten* is a flawless oracle."[11] Freylinghausen's opinion of

---

8. The Franckesche Stiftungen has two copies of Prüfung. One is a tract and the other is a chapter in a collection of materials put together for Breithaupt (AFSt 88K 30). The latter has a printed marginal note on section (44) that reads, "God's self passes judgment and reveals fully." All other marginal notes were contained within the tract and the other unusual feature is that the above is in a cursive script rather than the normal typeface. It is reasonable to assume that the author is the redactor, and Neumann's argument about three sources, God, man, and devil, continued to bother him.

9. Freylinghausen divides it into sections §I–XXVIII, to which he attaches 143 paragraphs, numerated comments ranging from one sentence to several pages. It amounts to forty-three pages in its tract form.

10. Freylinghausen, "bescheidenen Prüfung." Prüfung Des so genannten Unvorgreifflichen Gutachtens/ Welches (TIT.) Herr Caspar Neumann/." From the title page.

11. "Ein unvergreifflich Gutachen pflegt man zu heissen, das man

those who are the protagonists of this tale, the children themselves, is also immediately clear: they are the "awakened children," "from God," and "powerfully praying."[12] He reports his
motives as being from the heart. He sincerely loves the children,
and has written it "in the fear of the Lord."[13]

In reference to what Neumann had stated, "A few weeks
back I said in my pulpit in the house of the Lord, it is spoken
very much today in Silesia of the praying children; I wish to
say therefore at this time, that GOD intends to judge this work
and reveal whether it is of Him or from man?," Freylinghausen
stated, "This is the chief key point."[14] This is indeed the key for
Freylinghausen, on which everything truly depends, whether
one judges this work through rational principles, or traces it to
its source and beginning. For Freylinghausen, forming a correct
judgment required understanding the time, place, and circum-
stances that gave rise to the revival. All depended on asking
whether God or man was the author and originator of it.[15]

---

niemanden als ein unfehlbar, und untrügliches *Oraculum* auffbürden /
sondern dagegen man vielmehr das *Judicium rectius sentientium* gelten
lassen will." Ibid., 2.

12. "Dieser von GOtt zum öffentlichen Gebet kräfftig erweckten
Kinder." Ibid., title page.

13. This is a very common expression of the period. Neumann wrote
his Gutachten , "In der Furcht des Herrn abgefasset."

14. "Vor einigen Wochen sagte ich in dem Hause des Herren, auf
meiner Cantzel/ ietzund rede man in Schlesien gar viel, von betenden
Kindern; wünschete aber damals, GOTT wolle selber dieses Werk richten
und offenbaren, ob es von Ihm sey, oder von Menschen?" Ibid., 3.

15. "Diß ist der eigentliche *Status quaestionis*, oder die Sache davon
gefraget wird, ja davon auch hauptfächlich und zu erst gefraget werden
muß: nemlich : Ob man dieses Werck ratione principii, oder nach
seinem ersten Ursprung und Anfang , als Göttlich oder Menschlich
anzusehen habe? Ob GOTT oder ein Mensch *Auchtor* und Uhrheber
davon sey? sintemahl hievon die Entscheidung der übrigen Fragen, z.e.,
was draus werden könne? was man dabey zu thun habe? gantz und gar

Freylinghausen believed that Neumann asked the right question, whether the revival was from God or man, but was not in the position to judge because he was not asking from the heart but only *pro forma*.[16] In other words, he was saying that Neumann was insincere. We have before us, therefore, a Pietist critique of both Lutheran Orthodoxy and early Enlightenment thought as well as a serious charge. Freylinghausen ended this section saying that he doubted that Neumann ever got an answer from God because he was only pretending to ask.[17] In the following section Freylinghausen objected to the Neumann's repeated use of the word "rebellion" (*Aufstand*) for an awakening movement and his later usage of the terms "confusion," "tumult," and "riot." The terms reveal the divergent interpretations of the revival between Lutheran Orthodoxy and Pietists.

Freylinghausen takes exception to Neumann's use of *Aufstand* early in *Prüfung*:

> With this designation [rebellion] which he hatefully repeats several times in synonyms such as insurrection, civil disobedience, to dominate, agitation, the tumults of the people, etc., Herr Author[18] explains one way but gives away his great hatred and indignation therein, how he has considered this work from beginning, so that one

---

dependiert." Ibid.

16. "Was nun auff den vom Herrn *Auchtore* selbst formierten *statum quaestionis* eigentlich zu antworten sey, muß ihm damals, als er hievon auf seiner Cantzel Erwehnung gethan , noch nicht *liquid* gewesen seyn; Weil sonst der gethane Wunsch, daß es Gott offenbahren möchte , nicht von Hertzen, sondern nur *pro forma* geschehen seyn würde." Ibid., 5 (1).

17. "Womit er also selbst deutlich genug zu verstehen giebt, daß er nicht aus Göttlicher Offenbahrung, sondern in unverantwortlicher Ubereilung diß sein Gutachen gestellet habe / oder die Göttliche Offenbahrung nur zum Schein gewünschet haben müsse." Ibid., 5–6.

18. Freylinghausen addresses Neumann by this designation consistently.

must wonder with such matters, if knowing a divine revelation of the thing was particularly desired.[19]

Not only were more and more children awakening as the movement spread, but many adults in the crowds who gathered to watch them were weeping, reflecting, repenting, and being awakened. Freylinghausen reasoned that if these prayer meetings became understood as rebellions they would not be comprehended as being from God, but from man or the devil, hence they would be rejected, which gets to his central point— that God was using these children for a very special purpose. It seems that "from the heart" for Freylinghausen also meant open to the work being from God. Freylinghausen believed the praying children were a sign that God was doing something new and this was the first dramatic sign that God was bringing better times for the Church (Chiliasm). (Freylinghausen's interest here brings to the foreground the connection between the ongoing Silesian apocalyptic current's affinity with this aspect of Spener's influential writings.) He saw the regenerating work of the Holy Spirit working on a mass scale. He also believed that the prayers of the children had power to awaken people and suspected the prayers had power in the supernatural battle between good and evil, though he did not develop this idea or others nearly to the extent that Petersen did.

Neumann's interesting choice of words was raised in paragraph §.II (4), "Why 'consternation'? Why not much more

19. "Mit dieser Benennung, welche mehrmahls wiederhohlet / und durch die gehässig Synonyma, Empörungen, Ungehorsam / Herrschen / Erregung des Volcks / tumultuiren / u.f.f. erkläret wird/ verräth der Herr *Auchtor* auf einmahl seinen grossen Haß und Unwillen/ darinn er von Anfang dieses Werck angesehen hat/ daß man sich wundern muß/ wie er bey solcher Bewandnüß erst eine besondere Göttliche Offenbahrung hat wünschen können/ was von der Sache zu urtheilen sey." Ibid., 6 (3).

call it: 'To our great joy and amazement?'"[20] In §.IV (17) he states, "It should be called 'movement' and 'awakening,' not 'indignation.'" He asks, "Then against whom are they indignant?"[21] Freylinghausen's question is political, practical, and pastoral: while new religious freedoms had been granted officially, the fact was the Silesians were still living under the Hapsburgs, and the authorities still had the power for brutal repression. He warned that when such arguments were heard the authorities could use Neumann's words indicating confusion, tumult, and riot to persecute the people further. This argument proved prescient considering how six Pietist pastors and teachers were in fact exiled from Silesia in 1730. Catholic authorities working with Lutheran Orthodox clergy used Pietist conventicles as their proof that Pietists were not really Lutherans and therefore they had no standing or rights under the Treaty of Westphalia. Freylinghausen made an ironic biblical observation that Breslau was a capital city and it was in another capital where Herod turned on the innocent children. He had raised concerns that other terms Neumann used, such as "scold" (*schilt*), showed that Neumann not only misunderstood the Kinderbeten but actually "broods against it." He said Neumann misunderstood because his mind was "asleep" (*betäuber*), which would suggest a state opposite that of being "awakened."

In sections §.III and IV, Freylinghausen gave some of the historical details of the Kinderbeten movement and in §.VI he answered Neumann's concern that the matter was being written about in so many newspapers even beyond Silesia with, "It would irresponsible if this wonderful episode should be omitted from histories and become absorbed by less important things, and future generations be deprived of the praise belonging to

20. "Warum Bestürtzung ? warum heißtz nicht vielmehr: *Zu unserer grossen Freude und Verwunderung?*" Ibid., 7 (4).

21. "Bewegung und Erweckung solte es heissen / nicht Empörung. Denn wider wem haben sie sich empöret?" Ibid., 8 (17).

God."[22] There was a similar concern here for history and posterity (*Nachkommen*) as expressed in *Die Macht der Kinder* and *Gründliche Nachrichten.*

Sections §.VII to XIII contain questions that the two men differ on theologically, *casus mixtus*. (This issue still generates interest with Christians). It seems reasonable to guess that Neumann had been asked for his opinion on this movement that had been the talk of the Breslau community for several weeks. Neumann reported that people were giving different opinions about the revival, and after reflecting on it, he had devised an interesting argument around the three ways of looking at it. The first was that it was a thing from God. The second was, "The whole thing is a work of man" (mainly the children were playing "copy-cat" as they saw the Swedish soldiers doing the same thing).[23] The third was a work of the devil. Neumann said that these were his same questions.[24] He compared it to three strands, embellishing his metaphor a little by speaking of golden threads and pearls (one assumes the cord of the devil was not golden and had no jewels). On one hand, his argument seems rational

22. "Es wäre auch unverantworlich, wenn diese wunderbahre Begebenheiten in den Chronicken, denen man wohl Dinge von geringerer Erheblichkeit einverleibet, solten ausgelassen, und GOtt der HErr seines Lobes bey der Nach=welt darüber beraubet werden. " Ibid., 9 (27).

23. The term used means "monkey-game" (*Affenspiel*) but is equivalent to our expression "copy-cat" though we up to recent times did have the saying, "Monkey see, monkey do."

24. "Ein Theil erhebet die Sache biß in den Himmel, und spricht: Das ist vom Herren geschehen, und ist ein Wunder für unsern Augen . . . Andere lachen zu dem gantzen Handel/ und sprechen/ es sei Menschen = Werck . . . Der dritte Hauffe schreyet: Das ist recht Teufels = Werk: Der böse Feind hat diese Quakerey erdacht/ Unruh in unserm Lande damit anzurichten/ und unserer Kirche einen bösen Namen zu machen . . . Der selben ihre Anfage ist mein Grund, den ich habe, und dar nach richte ich." Neumann, ibid., 10–12, §.VII, VIII, IX,.XI.

and reasonable and variations on it are still heard in Christian apologetics as people try and make sense of perplexing events, but it was too rational for Freylinghausen, who wrote some of his longest comments here, asking basically, "How can God be mixed with the devil?" His appraisal was, "The first is good and Christian, the other injudicious and immoral, and the last clearly godless, pharisaic, and of the antichrist."[25] God is like light and the other two are like darkness, so how does one mix light with darkness? What does justice have to do with injustice?

Freylinghausen's point was that Neumann had set up the questions in such a way as to necessarily find something wrong with the revival. Neumann's argument also contained the words, "The devil has his claws in the movement, intervening in everything," so even if God had meant it for good, the result was a mess. Freylinghausen was having none of this and took it on with many points in sections §.VII to XIII and continued raising many arguments on this point throughout the paper. He took exception to the idea that the children played "monkey see, monkey do" (*Affenspiel*). This, of course, concerned the revival's origin, a principal point of his:

> Whether the revival of the Silesian children with such an exceptional love for praying that they forget everything including sleeping and eating, show such great patience and unchanging constancy even in the frost and cold, their conduct in praying is so modest, calm, and in good order, these otherwise rough and wild youth have such willing obedience and a special devotion with tears, fear and anxiety for some until they become nearly unconscious, according to an amazing understanding, they have such an outrageous zeal if they had been prevented at the prayer, and so before Herr Author's eyes these

25. "Das erste ist gut und christlich, das andere unvernünfftig und liederlich, und das letzte offenbar gottloß, pharisäisch und Antichristlich." Freylinghausen, ibid., 13 (43).

entirely foreign things are either from God, or from man, or from the devil? I say that this is the main thing and calls all into question, how all three could be from the origin? Rather they are from the externals . . . From this mix it is impossible that something good could have been born and with this one seeks to justify and see what we want to see, this argument stands on very weak feet.[26]

Freylinghausen also had a real problem with the language used in §. XIV and XV that the movement was a "fate (judgment) of God (divine visitation), who has afflicted our homeland (Silesia)" (*Verhängniß von GOTT der unser Vaterland heimsuchet*).[27] For example, to say "to ravage a country" would be "*ein Land*

26. "Ob die erweckung der Schlesischen Kinder zu einer so ungemeinen Liebe des Gebets, das sie auch Schlaffen und Essen drüber vergessen/ zu der so grossen Geduld und unveränderten Beständigkeit in Forst und Kälte/ zu der so guten Bescheidenheit/ Stille und Ordnung / zu so willigem Gehorsam und sonderlicher Andacht/ zu so wunderns=wurdiger Verantwortung und Verstande/ ihres Thuns halber Rechenschafft zu geben/ zu dem unerhörten Eyfer/ Thränen/ Angst und Bangigkeit/ so sich bey einigen bis zur Ohnmacht vergrössert/ wenn sie am Gebet verhindert worden, und zu andern bey der sonst rohen und wilden Jugend ungewohnten/ und vor den Augen des HErrn Autoris selbst gantz fremden Dingen/ von GOtt/ oder von Menschen/ oder vom Teufel sey? ich sage / diß ist die Sache/ die eigentlich *in quaestionem* komt, wie den auch alle drey Urtheile vom principio, oder dem Ursprung/ nicht aber von *externis accidentibus,* oder ausserlichen zufälligen Dingen des Wercks reden. Wie kan man darum alle drey urthele/ die/ nach/ ihrem Argument und Inhalt einander nicht subordiniret sondern schnur stracks einander entgegen sind/ zusammen nehmen/ und daraus ein gantzes machen? Aus dieser mixtur kan unmöglich was gutes gebohren werden/ und stehet der Beweiß/ damit **man solche** zu rechtfertigen suchet/ wie wir sehen wollen/ gewiß auf sehr schwachen Füssen." Ibid.

27. It is strange language to use: "Verhängniß" means "catastrophe," or "doom." "Heimsuchet" means "to afflict," "distress," "to haunt," but was also used in the sense that Silesia was oppressed.

heimsuchen." Freylinghausen made the observation, "Divine visitations happen either in grace or in wrath . . . all faithful Christians see the visitations of the first type . . . [Neumann] sees it as the latter, it is a great blindness and for him it cannot be good."[28] *Ad hominem* attacks were common at this time, and Freylinghausen used them frequently, i.e., answering, "Why use such language?" with, "Because he is blind."

At this point in his message Neumann claimed God was judging Silesia through the work. He also attributed the prayers to God and detailed what was good and remarkable about the children themselves, stating, "No one with all his skills would be able to bring about that kind of uprising of prayer."[29] Does he contradict himself here? Certainly Freylinghausen argues so. Neumann did not have to be contradicting himself here if he meant that the form of the revival was a judgment on Silesia (the fact that it took place outdoors by children) while the mode of the children's worship (prayer) was something positive.

Why such a difference of interpretation of the praying children? Freylinghausen was almost archetypical of the Spener-Francke movement. Neumann was representative of both Lutheran Orthodoxy and the early Enlightenment (*Frühaufklärung*), neither of which took any interest in promoting the supernatural

---

28. "Die Göttlichen Heimsuchungen geschehen entweder in Gnaden oder im Zorn. Was gegenwärtige Sache anlanget/ so sehen alle fromme Christen dieselbe billich an / für eine Heimsuchungen erster Art/ die aus Gnaden geschehen über das gute Schlesien. Das sie aber der Herr Auctor für eine Heimsuchung der andern Art hält/ wie er mehr als zu deutlich an den Tag legt/ zeuget/ wenn man die Wahrheit bekennen soll / von einer großen Blindheit/ und kan für ihn nicht gut seyn." Freylinghausen, ibid., 19, (54).

29. "Da sonst alle Kinder, mit vieler Mühe zum Gebeth müssen getrieben werden. (57) Diese Sache ist so schwer und widersinnisch/ daß kein Mensch/ (58) mit allen seinen Künsten / (59) einen dergleichen Auffstand zum Gebet würde haben können zuwege bringen/ wenn es ihm gleich wäre befohlen gewesen." Ibid., 18.

beyond the need to apprehend it and believe it intellectually. It was not that Francke and Halle were not keenly interested in the intellect; they were part of scientific and scholarly advances. Where Pietism veered from Lutheran Orthodoxy was primarily the matter of experiential religion. Orthodoxy was a reformation of thought, and foremost importance was given to keeping the gospel pure by safeguarding teaching. Intellectual understanding was everything, and there was nothing to be gained and much to lose in any promotion of lay spirituality beyond the proper passive reception of the word and sacrament. Luther's teaching on the regenerative work of the Holy Spirit was confined to the means of grace, and for most Lutherans it remains the same today. Additionally, as the Enlightenment thinking spread among intellectuals there was little interest shown besides scorn for discussion of the supernatural. Such beliefs were based on superstition. Yet, among people in general, more so among Pietists, especially among radical Pietists like the Petersens, there was great interest in the supernatural. Not only did the Kinderbeten story become known through Europe and the colonies, but there was also a general interest in reports of children having dreams and visions.

Prüfung shows that Halle was interested in the supernatural but not in diagramming it. Freylinghausen made succinct points about the supernatural. Whereas Petersen gave detailed exegesis to explain a thing, Freylinghausen was more likely to do it briefly with plain words. A good example is in (62) in a reply to Neumann's discussion of how unusual the children's devotion was: "Just for the sake of how unaccustomed one is with the cause of these things, one needs to look at it as the working of divine grace."[30] Once again, Freylinghausen was frustrated by Neumann's lack of appreciation of his own words. Neumann had

---

30. "Eben um dieser Ungewohnheit willen / hat man mit Ursach / diese Dinge/ als Göttliche Gnaden=wirckungen anzusehen." Freylinghausen, Ibid., 20 (62).

stated that the movement was obviously, "The work of the Holy Spirit and His workshop."[31] As Neumann neared the end of his report, before he damned the work with faint praise as it were, he stated that he refused to pronounce any further judgments on the work, which predictably exasperated Freylinghausen: "Above in §. XIV & XV, admittedly he mentioned the splendid characteristics of the divine finger; but he neither praised them for it in this *Gutachten*, but ceded the judgment of God and did not want to judge anything from it further."[32] In doing so, Neumann earned the name Sadducee from Freylinghausen, comparing this situation to the scene in Matthew 21.

Freylinghausen addressed a point Neumann raised on the part revivals play in the growth of the church. Neumann said, "It is almighty, and can gradually spreads itself from one place to the other through all of Christendom and all people; and that, not by loud Enthusiasts or direct promptings (*unmittelbare Eingebungen*)[33] from heaven;"[34] Direct inspiration is core

31. "Will also gern zulassen/ daß in so weit (67) der Heilige Geist sein Werk und seine Werkstatt hier auch haben könne." Neumann, Ibid., 22.

32. "Oben #XIV. XV hat er zwar die herrlichen Characteres des Göttlichen Fingers angeführt ; aber er hat sie ja weder daselbst noch sonst in diesem Gutachten dafür gepriesen/ sondern hat sie Gottes Gericht überlassen/ und davon nichts urtheilen wollen." Freylinghausen, Ibid., 24 (74).

33. "Direct promptings" represents a major point of contention for Lutherans but should be of interest to scholars of pentecostalisms. *Eingebungen* means "impulse," "inspiration," or "intuition," but one may wonder how this is different from the charismatic understanding of "word of knowledge." Neither Neumann nor Freylinghausen discussed the point at length. Freylinghausen merely noted that Neumann lumped divine manifestations with that which was most suspect and rejected everywhere.

34. "Allermassen auch das gantze Christenthum selber anders nicht ist/ als ein Sache/ die allmählich worden/ oder nach und nach sich verbrietet/ aus einem Ort in den andern: Und daß, nicht durch

to Lutheran arguments against Enthusiasm, and Freylinghausen refused to take the bait but rather addressed the issue of evangelism and called Neumann's understanding of how the Kingdom spreads Pelagian. For Freylinghausen, evangelism happens through the regenerative work of the Holy Spirit—that is, when the Holy Spirit resides in the believer:

> (73) Because of the propagation of Christianity happens through the revelation of the gospel in the power of the Spirit of Christ . . . Also, the imitation of Christ in man would not be a human but a divine work, not by human imitation but by the Holy Spirit resident in us and is able through the coming of this power and government.[35]

Neumann's view of evangelism was that it is gradual. Freylinghausen highlighted his response: "The whole of Christianity was nothing else than an object gradually spread from one place to other!"[36] He wrote that Neumann:

> Should not be so suspicious when the Lord will fulfill the grace word that he promised formerly through his prophet to our times, because he says: I will put my spirit sealing of all flesh and your sons and daughters

---

lauter *Enthusiasmus* oder Eingebung vom Himmel; sondern durch Nachahmungen und Vermittelungen der Menschen." Ibid., 24 (73).

35. Denn die Fortpflantzung des Christenthums ist durch die Offenbahrung der Evangelii und durch die Krafft des Geistes Christt geschehen. So ist ferner die Nachfolge Christi/ dazu sie vermahnet werden/ kein menschlich/ sondern ein Göttlich Werk/ dazu man nicht durch menschliche Nachahmung/ sondern durch den in uns wohnenden Heil. Geist/ und durch dessen Krafft und Regierung kommen und gelangen mag." Freylinghausen, ibid 24, (73).

36. *"Das gantze Christenthum sey anders nichts/ als eine Sache/ die allmahlich worden/ oder nach und nach aus einem Ort in andern sich verbreitet."* Freylinghausen, Ibid., 24 (70).

Joel)/Acts

shall prophesy, etc. . . . it is a strange and extraordinary gift of the Holy Spirit.[37]

Freylinghausen connected the Kinderbeten to Pentecost and saw the revival as a divine sign of the coming end times, reinforcing this with additional comments.[38]

To sum up this section on historical theological understandings by the two men, what were their explanations of the source and beginning of the revival? Neumann's view is easy to recap: the revival began in the mountains and after December 28, spread from district to district. Its source seemed to be of God, but it had human and demonic sources at work in it. The devil was doing much harm, and one of Satan's strategies was to make this thing newsworthy and have many adults come, view it, and ruin it with their silliness. Neumann's strategy was to let it run its course and in the meantime put it under the control of clergy and move it inside the church buildings where it could be "baptized" and turned into a large Confirmation class.[39]

Freylinghausen was much, much more interested in the source of the revival; he said this was everything. For him the question was: how can something be both of God and of man and of the devil? He contested Neumann's three-strand theory. He contested the idea that viewing the Swedish soldiers at morning

37. "Solte ein solcher dazu ungütig und scheel sehen/ wenn der HErr auch zu unsern Zeiten das gnäde Wort daß er ehmals durch seinen Propheten geredet hat/ erfüllen wolte/da er spricht: Ich will meinen Geist ausgiessen über alles Fleisch/ und euer Söhne und Töchter sollen weissagen u.s.f. Weissagen aber heist/ nach dem *stylo* der Schrifft offt so viel als Predigen; oder bedeutet eine sonderbare und ausserordentliche Gabe des H. Geistes." Freylinghausen, Ibid., 36–7 (104).

38. "Das Werck/ davon die Rede ist/ ist selbst ein grosses Zeichen und Wunder unserer Zeit." Freylinghausen, Ibid., 37 (106).

39. See Ward. In some ways this was what happened to the Kinderbeten, though, of course, the revival continued for decades and there were reports of further Kinderbeten up to the Prussian invasion.

and evening prayer was the sole source, posing a few obvious questions. For example, he asked, "The Swedes were situated a whole year in Saxony and also held public prayer hours as in Silesia; why did the Saxon youth not [do the same]?"[40] He gave the source plainly: "I carry no reservations to say this prayer of the children is from divine effect, more good is present then at most so-called churchly worship services where certainly great frigidness and lukewarmness has taken hold."[41]

DIE MACHT DER KINDER

Petersen is considered a radical Pietist instead of a mainstream Halle Pietist here because he was not committed to working within the Church. Francke had made it clear he expected the renewal to come through the church. After all, Spener spoke of better times for the Church, not better times for true believers. Radicals were generally separatists, and that group as a rule, gave up on all who were firmly tied to the Church in the run-up to the millennium.

Petersen's title, *Die Macht der Kinder*, was his assessment that God's power and purpose was in the children's prayers. Their activity was a sign from God that the day of the Lord was at hand. The Spirit was on them, and the divine remained in them and their work. He saw many things in it; one of the hopeful things was that God was giving the world another chance. If Petersen was a journalist, he would never bury the lead: the introduction

40. "Die Schweden haben ein gantzes Jahr in Sachsen gelegen/ und auch da/ wie in Schlesien öffentliche Betstunden gehalten/ wie kommts/ daß nicht auch die Sächsische Jugend sich/ wie der Herr Auctor redet/ zum Gebet empöret hat?" Freylinghausen, ibid., 28 (78).

41. "Ich trage kein Bedencken/ zu sagen/ das bey diesem Gebet der Kinder aus Göttlicher Wirkung/ mehr Gutes vorhanden sey/ als bey den meisten so genannten kirchlichen Gottesdiensten/ dabey die grosse Kaltsinnigkeit und Lauichkeit gewiß mit Händen zugreiffen ist." Ibid., 34 (95).

stated that the children in Silesia were prophets, God's Spirit was at work in them to bring a revival, and most importantly, it was a sign to the world announcing the end times. Immediately following the acknowledgment of his patron, he stated his purpose:

> This world will need an uncommon love and veneration for God, and to cherish His Word, and the writing of His prophets, for the good of the Church, and especially of discerning the end times, so it is good to examine the present praying for the better future standing of the Church so to have discovered the meaning of when they are to come out of the wilderness; So the reason I have this present Tract is the uncommon movement of the prayer-driven children in Silesia, and the signs put forward in our present times out of the prophetical writings how such an extraordinary Awakening of the Silesian Praying Children. They are certainly forerunners of the approaching great and fearful day of the LORD, and are so rich, indeed the faith and youthful children of power because of their great righteousness, have been holding back the course so that He has not come yet, that the Enemy and the Avenger should exteminate as the destruction falls hard on the kingdoms of the earth.[42]

42. Petersen, *Die Macht der Kinder,* Preface 3, "Weil mir von vielen Jahren her nicht unbewust/ wie Ihro Hoch-Wohlgebohrne Excellence/ bey allen ihren hohen Affairen/ wozu sie in der Welt von den Grösten in dieser Welt sind gebrauchtet worden/ eine ungemeine Liebe und Veneration für GOTT/ und seinen Worte hegen/ und die Schriften der Propheten/ darinnen sie von denen *satis Ecclesiae* und sonderlich von den letzen Zeiten derselben geweissaget/ wohl untersuchet/ und so wohl den itzigen verderbeten/ als den kunftigen besseren Zustand der Kirchen/ wenn sie wie der aus der Wüsten herausgeht/ und sich auf ihren Freund lehnet gar deutlich gefunden haben; So habe im gegenwertegen Tractat, aus Veranlassung derer in der Schlesien mit ungemeiner Bewegung zum beten angetriebenen Kinder/ diese gegenwartige Zeit/ und deren Kennezeichen vorgestellet/ und aus den Schriften

For Petersen, the time was rapidly approaching when the "mystical Christ" would appear, and if the praying members of the Church could not discern it then the sighing of the children showed it. It was the time of the breaking of the sixth seal and the powers and principalities and the Antichrist and the Lord in the air.

Petersen stated that it was praiseworthy of Neumann to discern the finger of God in the Kinderbeten, but Neumann should not have used his preaching office in this way because it was clear that he neither understood nor spoke as he should of the event. The important thing was that God was at work in the children. Petersen drew on his own eye-witness account to claim that the children were at prayer before the Swedes marched through Silesia. He called their meetings the formation of little churches.[43] He played with the words "youth" and the term used

---

der Propheten gewiesen/ wie solche *extraordinaire* Erweckungen des Schlestschen Kinder=Gebets gewisse Vorboten des herannahenden grossen und erschrecklicken Tages des HERREN wären/ und so viel ben GOTT noch vermögten/ das sie ihn in dem Lauf seiner grossen Gerichte aufhielten/ das Er nicht komme/ und das Erdreich mit dem Bann schlage/ ja das eben das Gebet der gläubigen und unmündigen Kinder die Macht habe/ daß der Feind/ und der Rachgierige solle vertilget werden."

43. "Das man auch an widriger Seite so sehr bemühtet ist, das vornehmen, und Werk GOttes in den Schlesischen Kindern heimlich damit ümzuwerften, zu verkleinern, oder wohl gar zu vereitelen wenn man den Anfang der betenden Kinder dem Durchmarsch der Schwedischen Arme durch Nieder Schlesien zu schreibet/ solches kan man nicht billigen/ in dem ein gantzes Jahr vorher die Kinder zu Sagan schon ein dergleichen Vorspiel in Erbauung einer kleinen Kirchen/ die ich selbst gesehen/ gemachet/ und dabei sich versammlet/ und gebetet haben/ ob ich gleich nicht leugnen will/ daß die kinder durch die äusserliche *Devotion* der Schwedischen Soldaten nicht solten mit zum Gebet angezündet/ und man für gantz Göttliche zu sein nicht erkennen könnte/ so soll doch billig die göttliche Sache selbst/ die man von allen Partheyen freymüthig bekennet/ uns mehr dahin vermögen/ ein gutes/

in German for the end times, *Jüngste Tag*.[44] He stated Neumann should have understood and taken more care in his speech about how the power of God was at work in the children. He compared the Kinderbeten to Jacob struggling with the angel of the Lord in Genesis 32:28. This was an awakening, it was God's doing, and God's intention was a paradoxical reversal that the parents should be awakened through the testimony of the children, and it would lead to a good harmony. This is a fulfillment of a prophecy in Malachi,[45] akin to the work of John the Baptist, and fulfillment of future apocalyptic signs and the drawing near of destruction.[46]

---

als ein böses Urteil darüber zu fällen;" Ibid, Preface 5.

44. " Jüngste Tag": Ibid., "sich herunter zu lassen pflege/ also daß er nicht mehr göttlicher Kräfte annimmt/ als es die ertragen können/ in welcher Er/ und sein Geist würcket/ und deswegen in den Kindern/ so zu reden/ Kräfte der Kinder/ in den Jüngelingen Kräfte der Jüngelingen/ in den Männern Kräfte der Männer annimmt/ dabei doch alles/ in so weit es von ihm Göttlich ist und bleibet." See Gäbler, „Geschichte, Gegenwart, Zukunft," *Geschichte des Pietismus*, 4 Bde., Bd.3, Der Pietismus im neunzehnten und zwanzigsten Jahrhundert, 21.

45. Malachi 4:6: "He will turn the hearts of the fathers to their children, and the hearts of the children to their fathers; or else I will come and strike the land with a curse" (NIV). Malachi 4:6: „Der soll das Herz der Väter bekehren zu den Kindern und das Herz der Kinder zu ihren Vätern, daß ich nicht komme und das Erdreich mit dem Bann schlage" (Luther Bibel, 1545).

46. ". . . sie haben auch müssen die Weissagung des Propheten Malachia erfüllen der da weissaget, wie daß das Hertz der Väter zu den Kindern in der letzen Zeit, kurtz vor dem allgemeinen Bann der Erden, solle gewandt, und also die Eltern durch die Kinder, und nicht die Kinder durch die Eltern erwecket hernachmals aber wenn erst die Erweckung von Seiten der Kinder geschehen, auch die Hertzen der Kinder zu den Eltern gekehret, und in eine gute Harmonie solten gebracht werden, welches ich in den Werke selbst mit mehren ausgeführet, und gezeiget, denn zwar der Anfang der Erfüllung der Worte des Propheten Malachia im Johanne dem Täufer geschehen hen sen, aber zu gleich

To substantiate his claim that the revival was of divine origin, Petersen placed it in the larger context of Spirit-inspired movements in the church. This allowed Petersen to make comparisons that ultimately validated the revival while he also revealed misguided attitudes toward it (presumably like Neumann's). Petersen brought the child prophets of Cevannes into the discussion and also included the Inspired in London.[47] Therefore, Petersen should be understood as someone who kept abreast of the larger movement of people of the Spirit who were discerning the signs of things to come and as one who spoke of his own and his wife's experience of having dreams and visions (the dreaded "direct inspiration"). The Petersens were central figures in the German Philadelphian movement,[48] dispensational Pietists who were careful to attempt to demonstrate to the authorities that they remained in one of the two recognized Protestant churches, Reformed or Lutheran. Otherwise they faced expulsion for forming a new sect. The German Philadelphians' intention was not to separate but be "indifferent" to the *Landeskirche*, understanding it to be more important to network with others in what was essentially a communion of like-minded watchmen. They identified with the biblical community in Revelation 3 whose

---

dargethan, daß die gäntzliche Erfüllung in denen benden zukünftigen Apocalyptischen Zeugen solle erfüllet, und als denn dei Bann über die Erde gezogen werden, welches zur Zeit des Anfangs des Neuen Testaments nich geschehen ist." Ibid., 6.

47. After the Edict of Nantes, in the last days of the Huguenots' struggle in France, there arose a movement in which children were said to be prophesying by the Holy Spirit and they were even used by the Camisard generals. When these Huguenots fled to London they were known as "the Inspired." They were also known to exhibit physical manifestations. Petersen is the only person who brought them into the reports of the period, and he does so in passing as an indication that God seemed to be ushering in a new age.

48. See Gäbler, "Geschichte, Gegenwart, Zukunft," 25–9 and Schneider, *German Radical Pietism*, 21–25, 69–71.

reward for patient, prayerful endurance is the New Jerusalem coming down out of heaven and whom Christ will keep from the trial that is going to come upon the whole world.

Previous to the Silesian Kinderbeten, there were only two well-known incidents involving children in a religious mass movement: the Children's Crusade in the Middle Ages and the child prophets at the time of the Huguenot persecution. The former was not discussed in the writings of 1708/9, and Petersen was the only one to have brought in the latter. He called the Silesian children "child prophets."[49] The reason he was writing was that the sign was so important for his world, as well as posterity, but the reports and letters so far had not been convincing in themselves; one needed the Spirit of God to understand the sign. Before them was the fulfillment of the Prophet David in Psalm 8. These children were playing the same role as did the children in Jerusalem on Palm Sunday, shouting, "Hosanna, the Lord is coming."

After the preface, Petersen begins *Die Macht der Kinder* by saying it would be irresponsible to posterity for him not to write the book since much of what had been written already reflected a fear of the opinions of other people and had interpreted events as being under the influence of Enthusiasm or the devil himself, and so he went to Silesia for the express purpose of seeing it with his own eyes and giving a true report.[50] The work began through a special stimulation by God the Holy Spirit, and he said the movement had become entrenched and still contin-

49. ". . . so ist die Sache doch in den Augen Gottes so groß, daß er durch seine Propheten von denen Kindern zur letzen Zeit hat verkündigen . . ." Ibid., 7.

50. "So habe ich mir in Nahmen GOttes fürgenommen/ auf vorhergehende genaue/ und sichtbare Untersuchung/ der ich unter andern auch deswegen in Schlesien ausdücklich gereiset/ hievon einen wahren Bericht abzustatten." Ibid., 1.

ued.[51] Petersen used the same expression found in *Gründliche Nachrichten*, "While it may have originated from the observation of the Swedish soldiers . . . intelligent people are becoming able to see the special spiritual nature of the movement with the outstanding children's devotion."[52] He then stated the idea that is

51. ". . . so viel erlernet/ daß das Werck nicht ohne sonderbahre Anregung GOttes des heiliges Geistes angefangen/ und nach/als ich wieder heraus gereiset/ continuiret/ und forgesetzet worden sey." Ibid., 2.

52. "Man ist anfänglich auf die Gedancken kommen/ es hätten diese junge Leute/ bey Veranlassung der Convention zwischen Ihro Käyserlichen/ und Königlichen Majestin Schweden/ und der Wahrnehmung der Gebeter/welche die Schwedische Soldaten mitten im Felde gethan/ solchem löblichen Werck auch in ihrem Gebete nachkommen wollen; Wer will aber/ wie einer gar wol raisoniret/ zweiffeln / daß in dem bey den Kindern alles in so schöner Ordnung/ mit brünstigen Eyfer/ungeachtet all Hindernissen/ nicht allein beständig unterhalten wird/ sondern auch sich je länger je mehr ausbreitet / nicht bekennen/ daß es von einen höhern Treib/ als etwa die von den Schweden erlernete Gewonheit seyn mag/ ihren ersten Ursprung habe/ gestalt man den von so vielen verständigen Leuten/ so dieser aufgerichten Kinder=Andacht mit beygewohnet/ so viel glaubwürdiges hat/ daß es schwerlich/ ohne sonderbahre Gemüht=Bewegung/ angesehen werden könne." Ibid. Compare above to similar passage in *Gründlichen Nachrichten*, 4: Es mag auch wohl seyn / daß diese derer Schwedischen Troupen öffentliche Andacht zu dieser Kinder devotion die erste Gelegenheit und den ersten Antrieb gegeben; Wer will aber auch zweifeln/ daß sie/ indem bey derselben alles in so schöner Ordnung/ mit brünstigem Eyfer und eyfriger Andacht/ auch ungeachtet aller ihnen etwann/ wie vorher gedacht / sowol von der Obrigkeit/ als ihren Eltern/ deßfalls in Weg gelegter Hindernüsse / zugehet / und dieselbe nicht allein beständig unterhalten wird / sondern auch sich je länger je mehr ausbreitet / allermassen dergleichen nunmehro auch in denen Vorstädten zu Breslau / mit grosser Verwunderung gesehen wird/ nicht von einem höhern Treib/als etwann die von denen Schweden erlernete Gewonheit seyn mag / ihren ersten Ursprung habe / gestalt man denn von vielen verständigen Leuten / so dieser bisher erzehlten Kinder=Andacht mit beygewohnet / soviel glaubwürdiges Zeugnüß hat/ daß es schwerlich ohne sonderbare Gemüths Bewegung angesehen werden könne.

5dqs

found in all the reports (chapter 2 begins with it) that one needed to reflect on how it spread through Silesia in only five days.

In §. 2 Petersen says this holy and wonderworking God took the wisdom of these children and used it against the wisdom of the world. The children's hearts were simple and pure and through the Spirit's unction they had the wisdom to know what is hidden. It was wonderful that God's pleasure was to do great things through these small children.[53] He related the activity of the praying children to the angel serving at the golden altar in the presence of God.[54] Petersen made the point that other Pietists such as Francke and Freylinghausen made, that the testimony of children was special and deserved attention because their souls, while not without sin, were less complicated than adults. The title page of Freylinghausen's 1706 songbook had a drawing of children praising God (Ps 8), and in 1708 Francke was very interested in the visions of the young son of a German pastor.[55] Petersen quoted several figures, such as Bernard of Clairvaux, around the idea that the children have simplicity, innocence, and chastity. He expressed the sentiment heard elsewhere in the letters and reported that the children were like martyrs in the way they were criticized and treated, hence they were innocent lambs being led to the slaughter. He even brought

---

53. "Diesem heiligen und wunderbahren GOtt es oft gefallen/ nicht allein durch die mystisischen kleinen und unmündigen/ so bey Verleugnung aller eigenen hohen Welt=Weißhteit in der *elikeineia*, Einfältigkeit und Reinigkeit des Hertzens durch die Salbung des Geistes/ die Weißheit/ so im verborgen ist/ erkant haben / grosse Dinge zu thun/ und die Klugen der Welt damit zu Schanden zu machen / sondern es ist auch sein Wolgefallen gewesen / in denen Unmündigen an Jahren / und also warhaftig in kleinen Kindern/ wunderbarlich zu erscheinen / und durch sie zu wirken." Ibid., 4.

54. "Wer will diesen Kindern den Glantz abdisputiren / deren Engel allzeit das Angesicht ihres Himmilischen Vaters sehen?" Ibid.

55. The Francke archive for 1708 shows more correspondence with this pastor, J. E. von Exter, than anyone else.

up the old legend where Silesian children were slaughtered in the war with the Tartars in the 1200s and did not cry out but prayed for their murderers. Petersen pushed the idea that the testimony of children is an especially credible further witness, making a direct connection to heavenly activity. (It seems that when he does this he is also identifying his own Philadelphian community with the children and of course with Revelation and with the dispensation he has in mind.)

From sections 4 to 13, Petersen attempted to answer how the revival fit within the apocalyptic unfolding of God's plan. Therefore, we have an opportunity to study Petersen's specific premillennial view and its application in the relationship of the prayer being offered on earth to the events in heaven as told in scripture, mainly the events in the Revelation to John but also including many prophets and apostles and how those events in scripture are related to the events occurring on earth. Prayer always has power because it leads one before the face of God, but God is now revealing a special promise that has been in his word. The special stirring in Kinderbeten raised "an argument" that the fullness of the last days was before the gate, as it were. The King of glory was drawing near and the people were to become well-adorned bridesmaids or risk damnation if they were suspicious and rejected this special offer of grace.[56] The

56. "Wenn von der in der letzen Zeit zuvor gesagten Gnade des Gebeths so wohl der Alten als Jungen nichts in der H. Schrifft verheissen wäre doch das Gebeth Krafft des allgemeinen Befehls des im Geboth zu führenden Angesichtes GOttes jederzeit höchst nöthig auszuüben. Wenn aber nun eine besondere Verheissung/ davon durch die Offenbahrung GOttes in seinem Wort verhanden ist/ und als denn solcher Anfang/ und Anbrüche würcklich vor sich gehen / wer ist den so kühn / und verwegen daß er solches verlästere? in dem erheben durch dergleichen Regungen des H. Geistes das Argument nehmen solte / daß die Züge der letzten Zeit bereits vor der Thur wären/ und wir deswegen höchste Ursache hätten / dem herannahenden Könige der Ehren und würdiglich zu bereiten/ und als wohl geschmückte Bräute entgegen zu

seventh and eighth chapters of Revelation are central to his
argument. Of course, the context for this is the movement he
and his wife were part of, the Philadelphian community: "So we
are to become aware in the holy Apocalypse at the time from
the seven seals are broken and the seven trumpets are heard so
finds themselves that such should take place in the sixth mystical
Philadelphian community."[57] Christ would not come before the
appearance of the certain figures (or events that they signify) but
also not before his marriage to the community comes into being.
The prayers of the saints are an important component.[58]

We can take the list of texts in §.7 as an example of his
methodology: Revelation 7:6, 7, 14; 8:5, 10:9–10, 11:2–3. Why
Revelation 7:7, located in the middle of the list of the tribes of
Israel, is included in the list is seen in his reading of Malachi.

---

gehen/ daß aber solche Verheissungen in H. Schrifft liegen/ solches
muß ich aus einen und andern ort erweisen / Krafft welches Beweises
zugleich dargethan wird/ wie hart sich diejenige versündigen/ welche
eben das/ was GOtt in seinem Worte als eine besondere Gnade in der
letsen Zeit verheissen hat/ theils verdächtig machen / theils verwerffen
und verdammen." Petersen, *Die Macht der Kinder*, 9, §. 4.

57. ". . . also auch wir in der Heiligen Apocalypsi bemercken auf
die Zeit/ worinnen die sieben Siegel sollen gebrochen/ und die sieben
Posauner, gehöret werden/ so befindet sichs/ daß solches geschehen solle
in der sechsten Mystischen Philadelphischen Gemeine." Ibid., 10, §. 5.

58. "Klar ist/ daß der Tag Chrisit zu seinem Gerichte nicht eher
vorhanden sey/ es sey denn/ daß zuvor der Abfall komme/ und der
Mensch der Sünden/ und das Kind des Verderbens/ dessen der HErr ein
Ende machen wird/ durch die Erfahrung seiner Zunkunft/ offenbahret
werde/ und aber der Abfall/ und die Stunde der Versuchung/ so über
den gantzen Welt=Kreyß kommen wird/ einerley ist/ so siehet man/ daß
die Versiegelung/ und das Gebet aller Heiligen/ bey den erbrochenen
Siegeln/ und bey denen sieben Posaunen/ zur Zeit des zum gericht
herannahenden Lammes/ das nun als der Lowe aus den Stamm Juda
kömmt/ und ein Richter der Lebendigen und der Todten ist/ in der
Philadelphischen Gemeine vor sich gehen müsse." Ibid.

Petersen sees that the "twelve thousand from the tribe of Levi," is a type of the praying children. Malachi 4:5–6 states:

> Behold, I will send you Elijah the prophet before the great and awesome day of the LORD comes. And he will turn the hearts of fathers to their children and the hearts of children to their fathers, lest I come and strike the land with a decree of utter destruction.

This decree/destruction (*Bann*) is an important concept. The praying children were preventing this from being enacted and the "utter destruction" that would follow. Petersen gives the following texts as basis for role of the Kinderbeten prayer in end-time chronology: "These are the ones coming out of the great tribulation. They have washed their robes and made them white in the blood of the Lamb" (Rev 7:14). "Then the angel took the censer and filled it with fire from the altar and threw it on the earth, and there were peals of thunder, rumblings, flashes of lightning, and an earthquake. Now the seven angels who had the seven trumpets prepared to blow them" (Rev. 8:5–6). He also gave Revelation 11:2–3 and 10:9—11:1. His next at-length quote is Revelation 8:1–5. His interest is how prayers offered on earth have power to effect change.

> Another angel came and stood at the altar, having a golden censer; and there was given unto him much incense, that he should offer *it* with the prayers of all saints upon the golden altar which was before the throne. And the smoke of the incense, *which came* with the prayers of the saints, ascended up before God out of the angel's hand. And the angel took the censer, and filled it with fire of the altar, and cast *it* into the earth: and there were voices, and thunderings, and lightnings, and an earthquake.

Petersen's focus was the angel's offering of the prayers of the saints with the incense before the altar of God going up to the very presence of God, God's face, and how these prayers were followed with events on earth (voices, thunderings, lightnings, earthquake). In a prayer revival, those who are praying have influence on what is happening on earth because their prayers are offered at God's altar. Immediately following Revelation 8:1–5, Petersen wrote that if everyone in the Church would pray like the Silesian children prayed, the power of the common prayer would break the power of the enemies of God.

> If the prayer of all the saints was like that of the children in Silesia and if many congregations would begin to come together under the open sky, there would be are a good in-breaking almost the same as shots from a circle of wagons invoking God for their and all believers' protection; and the prayers is not about one or other community, rather as the Apocalyptic text calls it προσευχαῖς τῶν ἁγίων πάντων the prayers of all the holy ones on earth will be emitted together before the golden altar as the golden censer and coals of holy fire and smoke of the incense, this is the prayer are kindled by the holy fire and through Christ Jesus prove that his mighty power will not fall without effect on the earth that it is precisely because the voices and thunder and lightning and earthquake arise and the courts of the Lord break the power of the enemy and the avenger.[59]

59. "Wenn das Gebet aller Heiligen/ davon die Kinder in der Schlesien ein guter Anbruch seyn/ und in so vielen Gemeinen unter dem freyen Himmel zusammen kommen/ gleichsam einen Wagenburg schlagen/ und Gott zu ihrem und aller gläubigen Schutz erbitten/ erst recht wird angehen; und die Gebeter/ nicht etwa einer oder anderen Gemeinen/ sondern wie es in dem Apocalyptischen Text heisset προσευχαῖς τῶν ἁγίων πάντων die Gebeter aller Heiligen auf Erden zusammen stosten werden/ so wird das güldene Rauch=Faß/ und der güldene Altar/ vor desten heiligen Feuer/ und Kohlen der Rauch des Rauchwercks/ das ist/ das Gebet der Heiligen angezündet/ und durch Christum Jesum/ den seine völlige Kraft beweisen/ und nicht ohne Effect auf die Erde fallen/ daß eben dadurch die Stimmen/ und Donner/ und Blitzen/ und

Petersen clearly was teaching about breaking spiritual strongholds, pointing to the children as evidence of what God was doing and how they were a model for the rest of the Church. This is, "The power of the children." It is interesting to follow his choices of texts and his use of them as he explains biblical passages dealing with spiritual power of the saints: "Do ye not know that the saints shall judge the world?" (1 Cor 6:2). "And he that overcomes, and keeps my works unto the end, to him will I give power over the nations" (Rev 2:26). "I stirred up one from the north, and he has come, from the rising of the sun, and he shall call upon my name; he shall trample on rulers as on mortar, as the potter treads clay" (Isa 41:25). He also referenced Isaiah 26:1–6, which includes, "Open the gates, that the righteous nation that keeps faith may enter in." In reference to 2 Kings 2:9, he makes the point, "Who gave the Spirit when Elisha asked Elijah? Did not God do it? Should not God also be able to do the same thing in another time?"[60] In §.10, Petersen says that Joel 2:10–11 (the earth quakes, the heavens tremble) is the day described in Revelation 6 as the sixth seal and points to Revelation 19, Isaiah 13, 34, and 63, Jeremiah 30, Ezekiel 34, and Zephaniah, and says, "So it is clear that the great and fearful day of the Lord is the sixth seal."[61] He states, "We see that Pentecost has not been fulfilled fully because the youth had not prophesied! See Acts 2:16ff. This is being fulfilled now in the last days of the New Testament."[62]

Erdbebung entstehen/ und die Gerichte des Herrn über den Feind/ und den Rachgierigen einherbrechen." Ibid., 16, §. 7.

60. "Wer hat dem Eliä/ dem Thisbiten den Geist gegeben? Hat es nicht Gott gethan? Solte Gott denn auch nicht eben von demselbigen können?" Ibid., 22, §. 9.

61. "So ist klar/ daß das vorhergehende sechste Siegel . . ." Ibid., 26, §.10.

62. Ibid., 27.

The above was chosen from *Die Macht die Kinder* as an example of Petersen's interpretation as well as his methodology as a sample for a cross-section examination. His book contains many examples, explanations, and anecdotes that show Petersen was completely sure that the revival's origin was God. To summarize Petersen's argument, he uses an apocalyptic framework to interpret the revival, places the revival within the larger context of other revival movements to legitimize it, and believes God and His Spirit were working and having their way in the children, that God's intention was a paradoxical reversal that the parents should attain enlightenment through the testimony of their children and the children, are both a sign and a means of what God intends to do in the last days. God took the foolishness of these children and used it against the wisdom of the world, but more importantly, the prayers of the children had influence on what is happening on earth because their prayers were offered at God's altar. If everyone would pray like the Silesian children prayed, it would break the power of the enemies of God.

Freylinghausen likewise believed the revival had its origin in God, but unlike Petersen, he did not attempt to connect it with any other named movement or build an argument from scripture to explain why it was an apocalyptic sign. Rather, he trusted that it was from God, so even if the devil had his claws in it, nothing happened but what God allows, so the best thing to do about any untoward aspect was to take the good and trust that God would deal with the unexplainable aspects. Freylinghausen wrote, "The Holy Spirit's wonderful, real [physical], powerful effect in these children, is as the golden thread that runs throughout; and all parts are strung together on this whole string by his will."[63]

63. "Des. Heil. Geistes wunder=liebliche un kräfftige Würkung in diesen Kindern, als der güldene Faden, der durch diese gantze Schnur hindurch läufft/ und alle Theile zusammen heffet nach seinen Willen." Petersen, *Prüfung*, 14, (46).

Neumann, on the other hand, had many problems with the revival. In his *Gutachten* he would mention a practice, go to the Bible, and prove that this practice was no good. At each place Neumann did this, Freylinghausen would answer him with the same. For example, Neumann said praying outdoors was not good because Paul said "What! Do you not have houses to eat and drink in?" Freylinghausen refutes with, "The assembly the apostle warned of does not mean a certain place but the unity and community of the faithful." This back and forth goes on and on, and one of the things it shows is that there were two different interpretations of the revival.

It appears that the Lutheran clergy who were not Pietists overreacted to the revival as offending their sensibilities, that worship was to be inside a church building, not outdoors in the public. One might also guess that the clergy wished to have it inside where they could control it, and that is a hunch moving in the right direction. However, aesthetics or even perceived theological differences were not their only considerations. Their greater fear was another outbreak of Enthusiasm in their midst. To complicate the historical analysis is the factor concerning fear of a return to Hapsburg persecutions and the loss of recent gains in religious freedom. Fear of losing control was more than a perceived need. Crowds converging to watch the children would draw the attention of the authorities. Hence there were political as well as theological considerations. Concerning the theological, it is plain that from the time Luther left the Wartburg to expel the Zwickau prophets from Wittenberg, Lutheran clergy have been concerned by an entrance of any potential Enthusiasts. These concerns were never worked out—not in Silesia nor between Wittenberg and Halle. Within a few decades Lutheran Orthodoxy realized that the Enlightenment and Rationalism were the real enemy and laid their weapons aside as it were, but in Silesia they remained on the attack against Pietism, even to the point of using the Roman Catholics to expel the most successful

Pietist pastors in the revival. The conflict between Pietists and Lutheran Orthodoxy lasted in Silesia until the king of Prussia rendered it essentially moot in the invasion of the late 1730s.

The 1707–1708 Kinderbeten revival led to an increase of unsanctioned religious activity that was met by the anti-Pietist decree of 1712, the first of three edicts made before the invasion. In the following chapter we will conclude by looking at the specific complaints aimed at Pietists.

4

Conclusion

Previous chapters covered different interpretations of the Kinderbeten and how the revival reignited the controversy between Lutheran Orthodoxy and Pietists. It can be said that the children were both victims and pawns as they were censored and publicized. In order to get a true picture of the phenomenon, further research is necessary on the evangelische prayer meetings that took place in Hapsburg-occupied Silesian principalities prior to the revival. While it cannot be said that evangelische Silesian prayer meetings have been completely overlooked (e.g., the work of Herbert Patzelt) the alternative view put forward in this thesis is that the prayer meetings are the ✓ key to understanding the origins of what occurred in 1707, not the Swedish soldiers.

Even if it was not possible to prove that the Kinderbeten began in the *Gebirge* before the arrival of the soldiers, the importance of the existence of clandestine prayer meetings by the adults is indisputable. For the most part, these prayer meetings have been described as a coping strategy for the evangelische and a way of continuing their Protestant faith. The importance of prayer meetings as an outlet for expressing the need for freedom and that this would be something the youth of a nation would claim as their own has as yet not been fully appreciated. Furthermore, quite apart from any supernatural explanation, the significance of the motivation imparted upon participants of prayer meetings and reconsidering this as a force for social change could be another way forward for understanding revival movements without relying on a providential view of history. Overlooking the importance of prayer meetings is quite understandable; after all, prayer meetings are rarely the subject of detailed historical research.

It was quite the opposite in 1708. Prayer meetings were seen by Lutheran Orthodoxy and Pietist alike as having potential for change. Those in power generally viewed them as breeding grounds for unrest while those desiring change saw them as a tool for reform. Because the providential view was shared by all and it was assumed that God was the mover of history, they assumed some spiritual force was calling the children to prayer. Therefore, the possibility had been overlooked that when the children first began to meet to pray, they were availing themselves of one of the few means their disenfranchised parents had to seek change for things beyond their limitations—meeting with fellow believers to pray.

Prayer meetings were and are either controversial or misunderstood. The Kinderbeten phenomenon was essentially a series of prayer meetings, and this made them a conventicle in the eyes of Lutheran Orthodoxy who had been successful in rallying civil authorities to outlaw conventicles in some areas (e.g., in Leipzig in 1690). Conventicles became known as either an enemy of public order, or as it was for Pietists, a valued and necessary tool for Church reform, hence the controversy. Misunderstandings and mistrust over prayer meetings contributed to the mistrust of Pietism. While writing about Pietism in general, the chief spokesman for Lutheran Orthodoxy at the beginning of the eighteenth century, Valentin Löscher, wrote, "Pietism and pietists must not be rebuked as if they were public enemies of religion" and "the baby should not be thrown out with the bathwater." In fact, that seems to have happened over and over again.

Löscher himself seems to provide ammunition for this in calling conventicles one of the practices of pietism that makes it "a religious evil." That term is not far from an accurate description of how Pietism is still portrayed in North America. Representatives of Lutheran Orthodoxy continue to pass on Löscher's negative criticism and are silent on his positive evaluation. False pictures of Pietism are passed on to students in Lutheran seminaries in North America as they are routinely warned against it. Pietism is presented as though it had nothing to offer and made little contribution in the past, whereas the fact is the Pietists were the founders and the majority of pastors and congregations were Pietist from 1700 to the years immediately prior to the Civil War and with the wave of Scandinavian immigrants in the latter half of the nineteenth century the majority of the new congregations were also of Pietist origin. The patriarch of the American Lutheran Church, Henric Melchior Mühlenberg, was sent to the colonies by Gotthilf Francke of Halle. Mühlenberg referred to Halle continually as "the Fathers." As it was, Mühlenberg established the first lasting beachhead of Lutheranism in the colonies, and the Halle mission should get recognition for this. The absence of this recognition is an example of continuing negative bias.

As we have seen, the Kinderbeten revival opened up the old divisions between Lutheran Orthodoxy and Pietists. These divisions gave rise to competing interpretations of the revival, and the old divisions continue in the recirculation of false notions of the nature of Pietism and most likely the nature of Lutheran Orthodoxy. Leading scholars of German Pietism, such as Udo Sträter, have concluded that what is necessary at this point is a study of Lutheran Orthodoxy with similar intensity to which Pietism has had in Germany in the last few decades.[1] If we focused on the devotional writings of these figures rather than their polemics, how distinct would the lines be? If the theological difference between the two parties was great, how could they have joined together to fight the emergence of the

1. Personal conversation, September 11, 2008 with Udo Sträter.

Enlightenment?[2] Was it not for the most part the practices, rather than a different teaching of the Lutheran Confessions, that set Lutheran Orthodoxy apart from the Spener-Francke school of Pietism? Did not the Pietists' practice of meeting in small groups lead to most of the polarization? This is what is seen in the history of Pietism put forth by Valentin Löscher in *The Complete Timotheus Verinus*. He calls these meetings "the first characteristic of the present evil" and characterizes them as "disorder."[3] Löscher rightly displays his concern over practices that are not consistent with Lutheran theology and practice such as "scruples about joining a congregation" and notes that Spener condemns it too, but he repeatedly questions the sincerity, honesty, or frankness of Spener, thereby casting a shadow of suspicion over everything.[4] Why was the conventicle so roundly condemned by Löscher and virtually all of Lutheran Orthodoxy? Caspar Neumann said the children's prayer meetings were, "The work of the Holy Spirit and His workshop," [5] yet when the Kinderbeten began to pray in the open and without clergy supervision, this was so troublesome to most of the clergy that such meetings had to end, even if they had positive value. It seems that suspicion over what might happen, more than the actual practice, is what drove the condemnations.

Halle Pietism's interpretation of the Kinderbeten is certainly different from Lutheran Orthodoxy's. Halle thought it was an affirmation of the approach of better times for the Church, and this is seen in their republication of a tract Spener had written much earlier on prophecy and the jüngsten Tag.[6] The 1708 title

2. See "Historical Introduction" to Löscher, *The Complete Timotheus Verinus*, viii.

3. Löscher, *The Complete Timotheus Verinus*, 9.

4. Ibid, 16.

5. "Will also gern zulassen daß in so weit der Heilige Geist sein Werk und seine Werkstatt hier auch haben könne." Neumann, *Gutachten*, 11.

6. AFSt 55 K36. The title page reads, "H. D. Ph. J. S. Kräfftige und In

page of the re-publication states that the true Church of Christ had been patiently waiting for better times and the Silesian Kinderbeten was a sign of the change to come. Spener had elaborated there on Zechariah 14:7, "The night shall be like day." Interestingly, while Halle promoted the Kinderbeten in Silesia, they themselves did not promote an implementation of similar open meetings in Halle, which leads one to wonder if the group that is in power is always threatened by grassroots movements on their own turf.

Evangelicals abroad, as well as Pietists in Germany and Silesia, saw God's hand in every aspect of the revival. Rev. Schindlers of Silesian Lutheran Orthodoxy also used Zechariah 14:7 to describe the Kinderbeten, and he was certainly no Pietist. Silesians, Pietist and Orthodox, believed that the revival was providential, yet the revival opened up the old divisions, and not in an insignificant way. Orthodoxy wrote of the encroachment of Pietism as "the devil's claws." However, the Silesian evidence shows that what was being labeled heterodox by Orthodoxy was what people were doing, not deviations from Lutheran teaching.

When Orthodoxy gave its reasons for being unhappy with either certain elements present in the Kinderbeten or with Pietism in general, it was almost always a description of something that falls under, "We don't do it that way." Significantly, those who saw the revival as "from God but the devil has his claws in it" were the ones who pointed to "children playing copy-cat." Those who saw the Kinderbeten as an apocalyptic sign understood both the origin and the work itself as divine. Inflexible varieties of Lutheran Orthodoxy can give rise to a Lutheran Orthopraxy that insists if church practices are suddenly done differently it is assumed to be a sign of heterodoxy.

GOttes Wort fest gegründete Versicherung glücklich=besserer Zeiten/ Welche Die wahre Kirche Christi hinkunfftig zugewarten; Bey Dem Anlauff der in gantz Schlesien öffentlich betenden Kinder/ auffs neue angemercket. ANNO 1708."

One example of the old divisions between Lutheran Orthodoxy and Pietists is in a letter from Rev. Erdmann Neumeister of Silesia to Valentin Löscher. It shows that five months into the spread of the children's prayer he was more than a little apprehensive that Enthusiasm might be developing in Silesia. Neumeister was also investigating the theology of the young pastor Voigt who was sent from Halle to the Grace School at Teschen. In his cover letter for manuscripts submitted for Löscher's examination, Neumeister used the expression "the devil's claws" and wrote about a "red dragon concocting amazing public wickedness."[7] In his May 1, 1708, letter to Löscher, Neumeister referred to some pietists as "new holy and heavenly prophets," and concerning Voigt, "If he comes back, I will do my utmost to bring an investigation of his thoughts."[8] Voigt, one of A. H. Francke's handpicked students, was expelled by the authorities later that year with the reason given that the treaty stipulated that only Silesian pastors care for the Teschen Grace Church. This is an indication of the collusion that went on between Silesian Lutheran Orthodoxy and the Catholic authorities and what was to come in 1712 when the authorities (*Landesobrigkeit*) decreed that a warning against Pietism be read from every pulpit. One of the rights the Swedes negotiated at the Altranstädter Convention in 1707 was the reestablishment of an evangelische Consistory. This decree reads similar to the letters of Neumeister ("a particular people under the name of the Pietist known to externally confess our Augsburg Confession . . . which

7. "Es hat wohl ehedessen der rote Drachen sein Nest oeffentlich hier gehabt und den Terminismus ausgeheckt, welche Bosheit sich auch noch ziemlich reget."Wotschke, *Urkunden*, Neumeister aus Sorau 1 May 1708, 87–8.

8. "Es hat wohl ehedessen der rote Drachen sein Nest öffentlich hier gehabt und den Terminismus ausgeheckt, welche Bosheit sich auch noch zeimlich reget . . . Zugleich schickt er Loescher das Manuskript von einem „neuen Heiligen und himmlischen Propheten", dazu ein Buch des Pfarrers von Guetsenhain . . . ," Ibid.

we consistently find denied"). It appears that Lutheran Orthodox clergy used the Consistory to suppress Pietism even though they had only recently won limited religious freedom themselves.

It is clear from the 1712 decree that Orthodoxy's understanding of Confessional Lutheranism was being protected and the "foreign" one (Pietism) was targeted for extermination. The decree warned everyone to avoid "certain people who are called Pietists." It makes the charge that they only "externally confess our Augsburg Confession" serious because Pietists would have no legal protection without the status of belonging to the churches of the AC. The decree says the Pietists were "everywhere coming and going," and that the authorities were serving notice that they would no longer allow this "to be propagated."[9] The major alleged charges against the Pietists contained in this decree were that they taught direct inspiration (*unmittelbare Eingebung*), that one could become so perfect one did not need to go to Communion (*Stillestand*), that they had secret gatherings (*heimliche Winkelversammlungen*), and that there was going to be a new kingdom of Christ on earth (*Chiliasmus*). The *Landesobrigkeit* included the beliefs of Quakers, Schwenkfelders, and radical Pietists under a general umbrella of Pietism. They apparently intended to make a clean sweep. The decree ends with a warning for Pietists to leave. Any who stayed in Silesia would receive "well-deserved punishment" (*wohlverdienten Strafen*), as would any who allowed meetings in their home, provided them shelter, or had possession of their materials.[10]

Clergy who only a few years earlier were marginalized themselves colluded with the authorities to wield power over their opponents. It appears that their fear of losing control to enthusiasts led the orthodox clergy to exhibit an excessive spirit themselves! It should be mentioned here that there is little proof that there was a foundation for any of the charges stated above.

9. Meyer, *Gnadenfrei*, 21–3.
10. Ibid.

It was this same understanding, seizing on a religious meeting in a home, that led to the expulsion of Steinmetz in 1730. In other words, non-pietistic evangelische clergy would rather have seen an end to the most successful outreach witnessed in Silesia (Jesus Church in Teschen had a weekly attendance of forty thousand!) than have it be tinged with Pietism. A review of the reactions of the evangelische clergy to the Kinderbeten shows that the major objection of the Silesian clergy was that the praying was done outdoors and crowds would gather. As long as the praying was done in a church under supervision it was orthodox; otherwise it was "pietistic."[11] Rev. Schindlers wrote that a "certain man" said the Kinderbeten revival was "quakerish, pietistic, yes, heathenish." [12] According to Conrads, Schindler was the author of that report and probably held that belief himself. This is interesting because this letter is much more favorable than the longer one written by him a short while later, which is also included in *Gründliche Nachrichten*. This raises the question of why Schindlers quickly came to a harsher conclusion. The first letter states that "quite a few clergy" (*etliche Clerisey*) "rage against it horribly." Perhaps as soon as trouble developed with the growth of adult onlookers, he felt the need to denounce it, perhaps because of fear of Hapsburg reprisal. Conrads does not mention a political explanation, though, rather that the Silesian clergy disliked intruding Pietists, stating that young Pietists from Saxony and Prussia favored this unusual situation because they identified with the Kinderbeten and it was their visits and writing in support of the Kinderbeten that led to increased resistance from the Lutheran orthodox clergy.[13]

11. Conrads, *Altranstädter Convention*, 71.

12. Ibid.

13. "Mit einer ganzen Reihe ähnlicher Stimmen zusammen, liegt hier ein sehr erstaunlicher Beleg dafür vor, wie der aus Sachsen und Brandenburg herüberwehende junge Pietismus, begünstigt von einer religiös entzündbaren Ausnahmesituation, sich mit dem Kinderbeten

It is difficult to know exactly what motivated these negations of the Kinderbeten in print as well as the general denunciation of Pietists by Lutheran Orthodoxy; therefore, it seems that historians should be careful not to pass on the stereotypes that were incorrectly applied to Pietists in the past. Do we assume that Silesia was threatened by an invasion of Quakers sometime prior to 1712 because the threat was outlined in the Silesian anti-Pietist decree of that year? No, rather we should ask what motivated a reaction that seems intemperate and out-of-balance. People were meeting without clergy supervision, and for this they were labeled heretic? A huge prayer revival had broken out a few years earlier, which was like nothing they had seen before, and so devils and enthusiasts were projected upon it. What should Lutheran Orthodoxy have discerned emerging before their eyes? Was anything happening in conflict with the Augsburg Confession? Certainly nothing was being taught by these children. Why was it not seen that what was happening was a reemergence of the old Silesian desire for better days? The children had learned to pray from their parents and in the absence of regular catechesis some of the old mysticism may have crept in, but it is amazing that of Neumann, Schindler, or the six clergy who signed his letter, none made the connection that they were seeing the children take the clandestine worship public: the parents had hid in the forest to pray, but the children took it to the market square.[14]

What conflict was there in the theology behind the practices of this spirituality and the Lutheran Confessions? They had been evangelische for nearly two centuries and Hussite for

---

identifiziert, es aufgreift, organisiert und weiterverbreitet, bis es unter dem wachsenden Widerstand der lutherischen Orthodoxie in Frühjar 1708 verebbt und in mancherlei Unfug ausartet." Ibid.

14. The six were from various cities. They all seem to be eyewitnesses, and each added a few condemnatory sentences with only one stating, "We should wait and watch."

nearly a century before that. This "revolt" was a reemergence of lay piety that was being fed by Halle Pietism through edificatory tracts emphasizing biblical teaching. To discern what could be in conflict one would look at what had been present, what was being added to it, and what evidence there was of the final product. Which of these differences, either on the grounds of its theology or its practice, was in conflict with the Lutheran Confessions?

Three typical sources given for Silesian Pietism are the lay pietism initiated by Schwenkfeld, the radical mysticism of Jacob Böhme (1575–1623), and the "inner church mystic."[15] One cannot argue against these as significant influences, but what is the evidence that any of the children or the Silesian Pietist pastors taught or practiced mysticism during this period? If there were only five hundred Schwenkfelders at the time of the 1712 anti-Pietist decree, and they mainly lived in a few localities, it is reasonable to assume that many times the Schwenkfelder label was applied loosely and pejoratively to those who expressed themselves in ways that made Roman Catholics and Lutheran Orthodoxy uncomfortable. What evidence was there that "the radical mysticism of Jacob Böhme" or "the inner church mystic" was present in the children or any of the Silesian Pietists? Were these not only general influences in the background?

Of course, a strict Confessional Lutheran will find some points in the writings of radicals objectionable, but that is not the same thing as finding these things in what the children were doing, or what Pietist Silesian pastors were saying or doing. Schott's categories are reasonable; after all, Schwenkfeld (and Crautwald) and Böhme were some of the most influential, independent, radical writers in Protestant history, and they were born in Silesia. There is no denying their influence, but it is not safe to assume that they convinced evangelische Silesians to abandon

---

15. Schott, "Der Pietismus in Schlesien.," 129 (see chapter 1, note 25).

Lutheran teaching. Schott stated, "The radical Reformation's critique of the Catholic Church led to the concept that the real church (*ipso invisibilis*) was made up of true Christians, and that is based not on intellectual assent to a declaration of forgiveness but on being awakened and enlightened."[16]

Schott wrote "awakened and enlightened" without further explanation, and without knowing exactly what he meant, whatever being enlightened meant to Schwenkfelders, it is important to understand that being awakened or being enlightened did not begin with Schwenkfeld. They are terms taken from the Bible, and all Christians, before, during, and after the Reformation alike, use these terms. It is not as though Luther had not taught about "the new man" in the Small Catechism that "should come forth daily and rise up, cleansed and righteous,"[17] or that he did not tell of his own conversion in understanding as "being born again." Dividing the church into "visible and invisible" is shared by all Lutherans (as well as other traditions). Schwenkfeld was influenced by both Luther and Zwingli, *as were nearly everyone else*. More importantly, *everyone* at the time immediately preceding the Reformation was influenced by Late Middle Ages thought and mysticism. This is not to disagree with Schott's work, only to bring in an important consideration: the Reformation was not a clean break from what came before, especially in the faith of those who were not trained in the universities. All the elements of Pietism were present before the Reformation *and* in the teachings of Luther, Melanchthon, and all the Reformers. Halle Pietists consistently saw their project as another Reformation, a needed next step; the Reformation

16. "Die Radikalisierung der reformatorischen Kritik an der römischen Kirche zunächst mit dem Ziel der Etablierung einer von Erweckten und Erleuchteten, das meint: von wahren Christen, getragenen Laienkirche. Initiator und Wortführer dieser Bewegung war Caspar von Schwenkfeld." Schott, "Der Pietismus in Schlesien," 126.

17. Martin Luther, *Small Catechism*, 349.

of Luther was the reformation of thought and theirs was the reformation of life. The only additional consideration would be Spener's idea of "better days ahead for the life of the Church." This was seen by Lutheran Orthodoxy as in conflict with Article XVII of the Augsburg Confession, but as it has been pointed out, that may well be due to a sentiment that viewed any teaching that the Christ would rule a kingdom on earth as Jewish.[18]

Johannes Wallmann has stated that if one wants to know a movement one looks at the center, not at its edges.[19] Gottfried Arnold and the Petersens were definitely "edgy." Running through the pages of *Unschuldige Nachricht* in 1708 is a constant reappearance of these names as well as their critics. Löscher himself was drawn into a long battle with Joachim Lange. Much has been learned from the study of these figures, but the true nature of Pietism, Silesian or otherwise, has not. Pietist studies has been a continuation of thinking that one knows a period by its great men. Much is lost in the "Great Pietist vs. Great Orthodox" historiography, for example learning what caused the explosion of missionary energy in the Protestant church. Why did so many Pietists, and often lay people, desire to become missionaries, and why were so many from Silesia and Moravia? They were simple Christians with a Jesus piety. Good research remains to be done on what comprised the faith of these common people and how much influence it had on what was to come in the reformed *Brüder*-Unität at Herrnhut. Zinzendorf seems to be the major figure in all such studies, with not nearly as much research done into equally interesting people such as the layman Christian David. Regardless, it was the beliefs and the mindset of the common people that led to the strength of these movements, and we really do not know enough about them.

The Kinderbeten prayer revival did not come from nowhere: smaller prayer revivals had preceded it. Silesian Lutheran Pietist

18. See Gäbler, "Geschichte, Gegenwart, Zukunft."

19. See Wallmann, "Frömmigkeit und Gebet."

pastors like Schwedler, Sommer, and Opfergelt saw no conflict between their understanding of Lutheranism and the Augsburg Confession. It does not appear that they taught "direct inspiration" or "perfection" as the 1712 decree accused. They brought the awakened into the parish and catechized them. They did have an additional emphasis on prayer and prayed for God to come to their aid. An example of their expectation is seen in the letter from Pr Friedrich Opfergelt to Francke three years before the revival. He held hour-long prayer meetings at home and at church that were "not without noticeable blessings" and "God has himself already awakened his seed, wherefore with us, heartily praise him."[20] Even if adults redacted the intercessory prayers of the Kinderbeten, still many thousands in many places requested that more churches and more religious freedom would be given them based on that "which through your kindness we have presently received."[21] We see that the return of 10 percent of the churches was interpreted as giving way to a possibility of having more returned. The answer of one prayer gave hope that additional requests could be granted, and children in all of Silesia joined together to pray. That is probably the answer to why the prayer movement spread as it did: these children knew how to pray because many of them participated in prayer at home devotions.

If what the children were doing looked like morning prayer but it was even closer to the description of the clandestine prayer meetings, is it not reasonable to call into question the theory of the imitation of the Swedish soldiers as origin? The latter does not address the reports that the prayer movement began in the *Gebirge* even before the Swedish soldiers' arrival. If "many thousands knew" that these children's prayer meetings were going on for months before the surprise visit of the Swedes, the next step would be to in a general way see what can be learned

20. See note 66, chapter 1.
21. See note 67, chapter 1.

about Silesian evangelische prayer meetings in the principalities under Hapsburg censure. It would be very interesting to find sources for sermons and testimonies of this period and consider the evidence concerning the prayer meetings, the content of the dominant theology, and particularly concerning the hope the children had overheard or were taught directly by their parents, lay leaders, and the *Buschprediger*.

Descriptions of the prayer meetings and the texts of the prayers indicate that the Kinderbeten prayed similarly to how people in prayer meetings still pray, expressing their concerns and confessing their hope. The hope and prayer of the Silesian children are found in Jeremiah 29:11–14, which says that God has plans for wholeness and a hope for a future. They saw themselves oppressed and in exile, and the Lord could bring them back to a place of peace and freedom. The Silesian praying children are a noteworthy chapter in the early struggle for religious freedom in the modern era and deserve to be a model of how hope for positive social change can be realized through struggling together with unity in purpose.

Bibliography

LETTERS

ALMW/DHM/517:52 Johann Adam Steinmetz to Nikolaus Dal, Martin Bosse, Christian Friedrich Pressier and Christoph Theodosius Walther, 1730.

OTHER PRIMARY SOURCES

Anonymous, „Gründliche Nachrichten Von derer Evangelischen Schlesier Kinder Andacht/ Oder Denen/von denen Kindern in Schlesien/unter freyem Himmel/auf offenem Felde gehaltenen Bet=Stunden." (AFSt 121 A17).

Anonymous, *Euröpäische FAMA* indem 74, 114–34.

Freylinghausen, Johann Anastasius. „bescheidenen Prüfungen" (N.B., printed May 1, 1708, anonymously, both author and publishing house undisclosed).

Löscher, Valentin. *Unschuldige Nachrichten*, 1709, X, XI, XII, 34–7; 367–69.

———. *The Complete Timotheus Verinus.* Milwaukee: Northwestern Publishing House, 1998.

Ludolph, Heinrich Wilhelm. "Extract of a Credible Account Received out of Silesia Concerning the Children There in There [sic] Dayly Assemble to Worship God." Eintrag Einstück, AFSt/H D 23 b 15–6.

Neumann, Kaspar. „unvorgreifliches Gutachen," Breslau, March 1708.

Petersen, Johann Wilhelm. *Die Macht der Kinder in der Letzen Zeit, auf Veranlassung Der kleinen Prediger, oder, der betenden Kinder in Schlesien, aus der Heligen Aschrifft vorgestellet von Johann Wilhelm*

Petersen, der H. Schrifft D. Franckfurt und Leipzig, In Verlegung Samuel Heil und Joh. Gottfr. Liebezeits, 1709 (AFSt 159 K 32).

Scharffen, M. Gottfried Balthasar. „Die Andacht Betender Kinder in Schlesien/ Welche sie täglich unter freyem Himmel einige Zeit hier zu halten angefangen/ In bescheidener Prüfung aufrichtig gezeiget von M. Gottfried Balthasar Scharffen/ D.C.W. Itso abermal mit einem Anhange vermehrt gedruckt." Breslau/ und Leignits/ Zu finden bey Michael Rohrlachs seel. Wittih und Erben. 1708.

Schindlers, M. David. „Zuschrifft An die benachbarte Priesterschafft Um Einhaltung Des Zulauffs derer Kinder zum ausserordentlichen Gebet."

Spener, Phillip Jakob. „Kräfftige und In GOttes Wort fest gegründete Bersicherung glücklich=besserer Zeiten/ Welche Die wahre Kirche Christi hinkunfftig zugewarten; Bey Dem Anlauff der in gantz Schlesien öffentlich betenden Kinder/ auffs neue angemercket." ANNO 1708. (AFSt 55 K36).

SECONDARY

Christian David, Servant of the Lord, being a translation of the memoir of Christian David as written by Zinzendorf and translations of selected letters and reports written by Christian David or pertaining to him, Moravian Archives Publications, No. II, ed. Vernon H. Nelson, trans. Carl John Fliegel. Bethlehem: Archives of the Moravian Church, 1962.

Das Zeitalter des Pietismus, Ed. Martin Schmidt and Wilhelm Jannash. Bremen: Carl Schünemann Verlag, 1965.

Barthold, Friedrich Wilhelm. *Die Erweckten im protestantischen Deutschland.* Wissenschaftliche Buchgesellschaft, Darmstadt, 1968.

Beyreuther, Erich. *Die große Zinzendorf Trilogie.* Marburg an der Lahn: Verlag der Francke-Buchhandlung GmbH, 1998.

Conrads, Norbert. *Die Durchführung der Altranstädter Konvention in Schlesien.* Wien: Böhlau Verlag Köln, 1971.

Eberlein, Gerhard. „Die schlesischen Betekinder vom Jahre 1707/8." In: *Evangelisches Kirchenblatt für Schlesien. Zweite Jahrgang.* Liegnitz: Druck von Oscar Heimze, 1899.

Eberlein, Hellmut. *Schlesische Kirchengeschichte*, second edition. Ulm: Verlag "Unser Weg," 1962.

Gäbler, Ulrich. „Geschichte, Gegenwart, Zukunft" in *Geschichte des Pietismus*, 4 Bde., Bd.3, *Der Pietismus im neunzehnten und zwanzigsten Jahrhundert*, ed. von Hartmut Lehmann. Göttigen: Vandenhoeck & Ruprecht, 2000.

Haberland, Detlef, „Pietistitche Literatur in Schlesien-Forschungstand und-perspektiven," in Helmut Lehman, Thomas Müller-Bahlke, and Johannes Wallmann (editors) *Interdisziplinäre Pietismusforschung*, Vol 17/2. Tübingen: Verlag der Franckeschen Stiftungen Halle im Max Niemeyer Verlag, 2001.

Hutter-Wolandt, Ulrich. *Die evangelische Kirche Schlesiens im Wandel der Zeiten, Studien und Quellen zur Geschichte einer Territorial Kirche*, Dortmund: Forschungsstelle Ostmitteleuropa, 1991.

Meyer, Dietrich. „Der Einfluß des hallischen Pietismus auf Schlesien," Johannes Wallman und Udo Sträter, eds. *Halle und Osteuropa: Zur europäischen Australhlung des hallischen Pietismus*. Tübingen: Verlag der Franckeschen Stiftungen Halle im Max Niemeyer Verlag, 1998.

———. „Die Auswirkungen der Altranstädter Konvention auf die evangelische Kirche Schlesiens und die Bewegung der betenden Kinder" (to be released)

———. *Über Schlesien hinaus: Zur Kirchengeschicte in Mittleuropa. Festegabe für Herbert Patzelt zum 80. Geburstag,* eds. Dietrich Meyer, Christian-Erdmann Schott, und Karl Schwartz. Würzburg: Bergtadvertlag Wilhelm Gottlieb Korn GmbH, 2006.

Meyer, Gerhard. *Gnadenfrei*. Hamburg: Ludwig Appel Verlag, 1943.

Patzelt, Herbert. *Geschichte der Evangelischen Kirche in Österreichisch-Schlesien*. Dülmen: Laumann-Verlag, 1989.

———. *Pietismus im Teschener Schlesien*. Göttingen: Vandenhoeck & Ruprecht, 1969.

———. „Die böhmischen Brüder und ihre Beziehungen zu Deutschland. In: *Kirchen und Bekenntnisgruppen im Osten des Deutschen Reiches—Ihre Beziehungen zu Staat und Gesellschaft.* Zehn Beiträge, ed. Bernhardt Jähnig and Silke Spieler. Bonn: Kulturstiftung der deutschen Vertriebenen,1991, 47–69.

———. „Der schlesische Pietismus in den ersten Jahrzehnten des 18. Jahrhunders," *Jahrbuch für Schlesische Kirche und Kirchengeschichte,* eds. Gerhard Hultseh and Dietrich Meyer. Lubeck: Verlag „Unser Weg" 1985.

————. „Wirkungen des Pietismus in Schlesien," *Quellenbuch zur Geschichte der evangelischen Kirche in Schlesien*, Schriften des Bundesinstitutes für Ostdeutsche Kultur und Geschicte, Vol. 1, eds. Gustav Adolph Benrath, Ulrich Hutter-Wolgant, Dietrich Meyer, Ludwig Petry und Horst Weigelt. München: R. Oldenbourg Verlag, 1992.

Peschke, Erhard. *August Hermann Francke, Studein zur Theologie.* Berlin: Evangelische Verlagsanstalt GMbH., 1964.

Pawelitzki, Richard. „Das Schlesische Kinderbeten" In *Jahrbuch für Schlesische Kirche und Kirchengeschichte,* 65, 1986, 91–100.

Reichel, Hellmut. *David Nitschmann, Syndikus* Herausgegeben von: Moravian-Gesellschaft für Geschichte und Heimatkunde Suchdol nad Odrou, Band 16, 1 Auflage (no date or other publication data given, obtained at Herrnhut Archiv 9/15/08).

Schmid, Pia. „Die Kindererweckung in Herrnhut am 17. August 1727," *Neue Aspekte der Zinzendorf-Forschung.* Ed. Martin Brecht and Paul Peucker. Göttigen: Vandenhoeck & Ruprecht, 2006, S. 115–33 (Arbeiten zur Geschichte des Pietismus, Bd. 47).

————. „*Kinderkultur* als Forschungskonstrukt. Ein Ereignis aus dem Jahr 1727" In: Zeitschrift für Pädagogik. 52. Jg. 2006, Heft 1, S. 127–48.

Schmmelpfennig, C.A. „Zur Geschichte des Pietismus in Schlesien von 1707–1740, Von Dr. C. A. Schmmelpfennig, ev. Pfarrer in Arnsdorf." In *Zeitschrift des Vereins für Geschichte und Alterthum Schlesiens.* Namens des Vereins herausgegeben von Dr. Colmar Gruenhagen.Breslau, Joseph Mar and Komp,1868.

Schneider, Hans. *German Radical Pietism,* trans. Gerald T. MacDonald. Pietist and Wesleyan Studies, No. 22. Lanham, Maryland: Scarecrow Press, 2007.

Schott, Christian-Erdmann. „Der Pietismus in Schlesien" ed. Dietrich Meyer, Christian-Erdmann Schott and Karl Schwarz. In *Über Schlesien Hinaus: Zur Kirchengeschichte in Metteleuropa, Festgabe für Herbert Patzelt zum 80. Geburstag.* Würzburg: Bergtadtverlag Wilheml Gottlieb Korn GmbH, 2006.

———. „Caspar Neumans,Kern Aller Gebete' Zum 350. Geburtstag des Breslauer Kircheninspektors," *Jahrbuch für Schlesische Kirche und Kirchengeschichte* 76:77 (1197/8), 243–51.

Shantz. Douglas H. *Crautwald and Erasmus: A Study in Humanism and Radical Reform in Sixteenth Century Silesia*, Biblioteca Dissedentium, scripta et studia, No. 4. Baden-Baden: Editions Valentin Koerner, 1992.

Schwarz, Walter „August Hermann Francke und Schlesien," *Jahrbuch für Schlesische Kirche und Kirchengeschichte*, 1957.

Stoeffler, F. Ernest. *The Rise of Evangelical Pietism*. Leiden: Brill, 1965.

———. *German Pietism During the Eighteenth Century*, Leiden: Brill, 1973.

———. *Continental Pietism and Early American Christianity*, Grand Rapids, Michigan: Eerdmans, 1976.

Strom, Jonathon. "Problems and Promises of Pietism Research," *Church History*, 71:33, 536-554, American Society of Church History, 2002.

Wallmann, Johannes. *Der Pietismus*. Vandenhoeck & Rupert, 2005.

———. „Frömmigkeit und Gebet," in *Geschichte des Pietismus. 4*. Göttingen: Vandenhoeck & Ruprecht, 2004, 83–101.

———. *Halle und Osteuropa: Zur europäischen Austrahlung des hallischen Pietismus*. ed. Johannes Wallman and Udo Sträter. Tübingen Verlag der Franckeschen Stiftungen Halle im Max Niemeyer Verlag, 1998.

Winter, Eduard . *Die Plege der West-und Sued-Slavischen Sprachen in Halle im 18. Jahrhundert*. Berlin: Akademie-Verlag,1954.

Ward, W.R. *The Protestant Evangelical Awakening*. Cambridge: Cambridge Univ. Press, 1992.

———. "Bibliographical Survey, German Pietism, 1670–1750," *Journal of Ecclesiastical History* 44 (1993): 476–505.

———. "Review: Piety and Politics," *Pietismus und Neuzeit* 12, 1986, (Göttingen: Vandenhoeck & Ruprecht, 199–202.

Weigelt, Horst. *The Schwenkfelders in Silesia*, trans. Peter C. Erb. Pennsburg, PA: Schwenkfelder Library, 1985.

Westerkamp, Marilyn J. *Triumph of the Laity*. New York: Oxford University Press, 1988.

Wotschke, Theodor. „Urkunden zur Geschichte des Pietismus in Schlesien," *Jahrbuck des Bereins für Schlesische Kirchengeschichte XX*.

Band. Liegnitz: Oscar Hienze, Buchdruckerei und Verlagsanstalt, 1929, 58–129.

———. „Urkunden zur Geschichte des Pietismus in Schlesien" Sonder-abdruck aus dem *Jahrbuck des Bereins für Schlesische Kirchenge-schichte XXII. Band*. Oscar Hienze, Buchdruckerei und Verlagsan-stalt, Liegnitz,1931, 103–31.

———. „Leipziger Ordination für Schlesien," Leipzig: Oscar Heinzes Buchbruckerei, 1915.

Zimmerman, Hildegard. Caspar Neumann und die Enstehung der Frühaufklärung". Witten-Ruhr: Luther-Velag, 1969.

From a report on the Altranstädter Convention.

"gründlichen Nachrichten."
Courtesy of Franckesche Stiftungen, Halle, Germany.